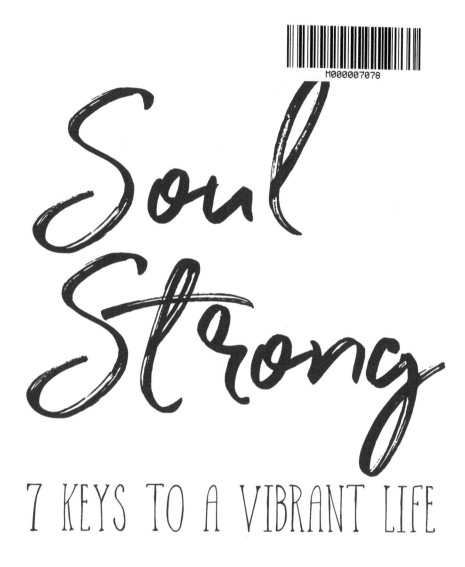

Soul Strong

7 KEYS TO A VIBRANT LIFE

Lucinda Secrest McDowell

NEW HOPE®
PUBLISHERS
Imprint of Iron Stream Media

Birmingham, AL

New Hope® Publishers
100 Missionary Ridge
Birmingham, AL 35242
NewHopePublishers.com
An imprint of Iron Stream Media
IronStreamMedia.com

New Hope Publishers serves its authors as they express their views, which may not express the views of the publisher.

Library of Congress Cataloging-in-Publication Data

Names: McDowell, Lucinda Secrest, 1953- author.
Title: Soul strong : 7 keys to a vibrant life / Lucinda Secrest McDowell.
Description: Birmingham, Alabama : New Hope Publishers, 2020.
Identifiers: LCCN 2019040303 (print) | LCCN 2019040304 (ebook) | ISBN 9781563093272 (trade paperback) | ISBN 9781563093289 (epub)
Subjects: LCSH: Christian life.
Classification: LCC BV4501.3 .M3264 2020 (print) | LCC BV4501.3 (ebook) | DDC 248.4--dc23
LC record available at https://lccn.loc.gov/2019040303
LC ebook record available at https://lccn.loc.gov/2019040304

ISBN-13: 978-1-56309-327-2
Ebook ISBN: 978-1-56309-328-9

1 2 3 4 5—24 23 22 21 20

For Daughters Everywhere,
Especially *Fiona* and *Maggie*

That day I turned around, and life had flown . . .
Whilst chasing dreams and children;
Both stumbling and soaring
in the search for holy significance.
Compassionately rescued from despair;
Gifted with a grace that accepts and extends;
Encouraged and loved.
Discovering serenity in silence,
and strength in surrender.
Filled, then poured out.
Heart broken, then mended.
Embracing creative words, life-giving music,
breathtaking beauty, and extraordinary people.
Walking with a limp, but still walking
Daily in God's presence and power.
Beloved.
Learning to love everybody always.
Not a perfect life, more a passionate pursuit.
Daughters, here is what I know for sure:
We can live *soul strong*.

—Lucinda Secrest McDowell

Other books from
Lucinda Secrest McDowell

Life-Giving Choices: 60 Days to What Matters Most
Ordinary Graces: Word Gifts for Any Season
Dwelling Places: Words to Live in Every Season
Refresh: A Spa for Your Soul
Live These Words: An Active Response to God

*To Kate
Happy birthday
♡ Colette 2020*

*for Kate –
Strength!*

I give you thanks, O LORD, with my whole heart;
    before the gods I sing your praise;
I bow down toward your holy temple
        and give thanks to your name for your steadfast love
        and your faithfulness . . .
On the day I called, you answered me;
    my *strength of soul* you increased.

—Psalm 138:1–3 ESV (emphasis added)

Lucinda Secrest McDowell

Contents

How Do You Do It?. xiii

CHAPTER 1: Live Loved 1
I believe I am loved completely by my Heavenly Father.

CHAPTER 2: Be Authentic 17
I discover and embrace my unique calling.

CHAPTER 3: Dwell Deep 45
I abide daily in God's presence, nourishing my soul.

CHAPTER 4: Pray Always 68
I live a praying life, bringing all to the God who answers.

CHAPTER 5: Overcome Pain 90
I allow my scars to open new doors of service.

CHAPTER 6: Extend Kindness 113
I become a person who freely shows grace and mercy to all.

CHAPTER 7: Share Stories 135
I reflect on God's faithfulness with gratitude and hope.

Why Do You Do It?. 156

About the Author. 161

Gratitudes. 163

Notes. 166

How Do You Do It?

*T*hroughout my life I've had many conversations with younger women. I treasure such experiences since I am constantly growing through contact with people from every age group. Recently, among the majestic California redwoods, one such encounter became the genesis of this book . . .

"Lucinda? I'm Kelsey; may I join you for coffee?"

I looked up at the young woman and welcomed her to my little table next to a roaring fire in the retreat center's coffee shop. "Sure."

"Thanks. I have so appreciated your teaching all week. I mean, especially about grace and stuff. This year I've been using one of your devotional books too and learned a lot."

"Kelsey, thank you for taking time to tell me. Your words mean so much, more than you can imagine," I replied with a bright smile.

"Well, actually, I do have a question . . ."

"Sure. Anything."

Her words tumbled out, "How do you do it? Be strong and faithful. Even when life goes crazy or you're exhausted and discouraged? How do you move beyond depression into hope? How do you keep going . . . for, like, *years*?"

"Wow. What good questions," I replied, practically on automatic. I gulped, and there was a long period of silence as I inwardly processed her question. *How do I do it? For heaven's sake, I don't even feel that I am doing it—living my crazy life—very well these days. Even this very minute I'm struggling with exhaustion, insecurity, and the fear of becoming obsolete. Lord, how do I answer this lovely young woman in a life-giving manner?*

I took a deep breath. "You know, Kelsey, your question is one I ask quite frequently of God. *How do I live this seemingly impossible life?*"

"And does He answer you? I mean, you seem to still be living and thriving even at your age . . . Sorry, I didn't exactly mean it that way."

Chuckling a bit, I assured her I understood. "He always answers but not necessarily with an audible voice," I said. "Over time in my seeking, answers just came—when I was reading a portion of Scripture or listening to biblical teaching like at our conference this week. I've also found guidance when people shared their life stories of overcoming obstacles. I realized that if God could help them, perhaps He could help me too. If they could be brave and steadfast, so could I!"

I looked deep into her eyes and wistfully revealed, "Honestly, I've learned the deepest lessons for living *soul strong* in the midst of defeat and brokenness. Those times God reached for me in His grace and mercy—lifting me up and setting me on a new path of hope and healing."

"Okay, so what did you *do*?" Kelsey kept pressing for something practical, "I mean, do you have a list or something I could go through?"

And I thought to myself, *what a perfect question.* A blueprint to follow. A list to check off. A reliable formula that if you do A, B, and C, then inevitably D happens. Only life isn't like that. Keeping rules perfectly does not always result in the predicted outcomes. Life is far more fluid. Messy. Occasionally it's gray instead of black and white.

Even as I sighed I felt a stirring of anticipation as well. "I don't have a formula or a list right now, but I have been thinking about such things for awhile," I told Kelsey. "I believe our journey of faith is actually 'a long obedience in the same direction.' It's not just a matter of physical perseverance or even mental determination. It's a deep commitment and an even deeper empowerment. I call it *soul strong*. But how that looks on a daily basis? I'd have to pray and ponder and get back to you on that, okay?"

"Sure," she replied as she finished her coffee. "But don't forget to email me."

"I'm pleased to continue this conversation as long as you realize that I'm no expert on holy living. I've made oodles of mistakes along my own journey, and I daily stand in need of God's grace and mercy."

"Well, that just means you're human like everyone else." No question there.

We parted ways and went to our workshops. But long after I returned home the conversation remained with me—a niggling and a nudge to put into words how I do it. I told God I wasn't qualified to write such things. Surely the keys to living *soul strong* should be presented from a place of great strength, not empowered weakness. Surely He has someone more visible and important to pass along wisdom. Well of course He does—many sisters. But as I prayed I knew that fact did not release me from obeying my own prompting from the Spirit.

I realized I might write more passionately if I made the search personal. So I asked myself what I would tell my own two daughters were they to ask me for my greatest life lessons. Opening a brand-new journal, my pen immediately began moving across the pages. When I was finished, I had a list of seven decisions I believe every woman must make in order to stay the course for a vibrant life. And in the past year, as I've researched and written this book, I've never even edited those original couplets.

What the psalmist declared in Psalm 138:3 (ESV) has also been my personal experience: "On the day I called, you answered me; my strength of soul you increased." Embracing these seven decisions has made me *soul strong* for the story God calls me to live:

Live loved.
Be authentic.
Dwell deep.
Pray always.
Overcome pain.
Extend kindness.
Share stories.

May I show you what I mean about seeking to live vibrantly and *soul strong*?

Chapter 1

Live Loved

*I believe I am loved completely
by my Heavenly Father.*

Deep in the Secrest family archives is an old reel-to-reel tape recording of little Cindy singing "Jesus Loves Me" with great gusto. I was two years old.

As I'm now watching my own grandchildren hit the two-year-old mark, I'm still amazed that a girl who learned those words at such a young age spent half a lifetime struggling to believe they were actually true.

Today when I sing, "Jesus loves me, this I know," I really *do* know it to be true—not only in my head but also in my heart.

My foundational identity is as the beloved of God.

I am loved by the creator and sustainer of the universe, the author and finisher of my faith, the great I Am, the alpha and omega—the beginning and the end.

This is where it begins, friend. The truth upon which all others stand: "Yes, Jesus loves me. The Bible tells me so."

So will I choose to identify as God's beloved? And thus live loved?

Will you?

This first, most significant decision will set the foundation. Who we are and where we are provides the trellis upon which to grow a vibrant life.

Knowing I am *already* loved, *already* accepted, *already* chosen, gives me both courage and confidence—empowering me to live *soul strong*.

> Jesus came to share his identity with you and to tell you that you are the beloved sons and daughters of God. . . . You were the beloved before your father, mother, brother, sister, or church loved you or hurt you. . . . God loved you before you were born, and God will love you after you die. . . . This is who you are whether you feel it or not.[1]

Do you know (in both your head and your heart) that you are God's beloved?

> If we really believed in God's love the way we are intended to believe it, we wouldn't be fearful under pressure, wouldn't compete wrongly with others, wouldn't covet, wouldn't strive with other people, wouldn't fear their promotion over ours, wouldn't be jealous of another. His love is unconditional. . . . We don't earn it. Don't deserve it.[2]

My favorite love verse in the Bible occurs when God's chosen people have (yet again) strayed far from Him. God reminds the Israelites of His great love for them through the words of His prophet Jeremiah, "I have loved you with an everlasting love; I have drawn you with unfailing kindness" (Jeremiah 31:3 NIV).

Perhaps you need that promise today. Circumstances of life have left you feeling trapped or unworthy or just far from the God who made you and loves you. *The Message* translation of Jeremiah 31:3 makes this even clearer: "GOD told them, 'I've never quit loving you and never will. Expect love, love, and more love!'"

Before making any important decision, it's always smart to do a bit of research. Examine these Scriptural promises of love, noting which words, phrases, or aspects of God's love are most assuring and hope-giving:

> Know therefore that the LORD your God is God; he is the faithful God, keeping his covenant of love to a thousand generations of those who love him and keep his commandments.
> —Deuteronomy 7:9 NIV

_____

_____

_____

_____

_____

> But you, Lord, are a compassionate and gracious God, slow to anger, abounding in love and faithfulness.
> —Psalm 86:15 NIV

_____

_____

_____

_____

_____

> The LORD your God is with you, the Mighty Warrior who saves. He will take great delight in you; in his love he will no longer rebuke you, but will rejoice over you with singing.
> —Zephaniah 3:17 NIV

_____

_____

_____

_____

_____

For God so loved the world that he gave his one and only Son, that whoever believes in him shall not perish but have eternal life.

—John 3:16 NIV

In all these things we are more than conquerors through him who loved us. For I am convinced that neither death nor life, neither angels nor demons, neither the present nor the future, nor any powers, neither height nor depth, nor anything else in all creation, will be able to separate us from the love of God that is in Christ Jesus our Lord.

—Romans 8:37–39 NIV

See what great love the Father has lavished on us, that we should be called children of God! And that is what we are!

—1 John 3:1 NIV

Dear friends, let us love one another, for love comes from God. Everyone who loves has been born of God and knows God. Whoever does not love does not know God, because God is love. This is how God showed his love among us: He sent his one and only Son into the world that we might live through him. This is love: not that we loved God, but that he loved us and sent his Son as an atoning sacrifice for our sins. Dear friends, since God so loved us, we also ought to love one another.

—1 John 4:7–11 NIV

_____

_____

_____

_____

_____

I hope you didn't skip over John 3:16, even though it may be so familiar to you that you know it by heart. Because that particular Scripture holds the key to the most important choice you will ever make. And that is simply, *if Jesus paid the ultimate price to die for me, then I will make the ultimate choice to live for Him.* For choosing our own way and not God's way (that's called sin), we deserve punishment. But in the ultimate sacrifice of love, Christ took that consequence upon Himself and died for us so that we might receive eternal life—living for Him now and into the life to come. The requirement is to believe in Him and to name Him as Savior and Lord before others.

Have you made that foundational choice—to enter the family of God? If not, or if you're simply not sure whether you have placed your faith in Jesus Christ, you can do that right now with this simple prayer:

Dear Jesus, thank You for loving me so much to sacrifice Your life for mine. I'm sorry I have sought to live by self-centered choices, resulting in sin against You. Please forgive me. Thank You for Your death and resurrection that I might live freely here and eternally with You in heaven. I invite you to make Your home in my heart and help me grow so I may serve and glorify You forever. Thank You for the great gift of salvation. For me. Today. Amen.

Receive the assurance that you are now and for always part of the family of God. Those seeds of faith planted throughout your life in various encounters are now blossoming into fruit through your new commitment to trust Christ as both Savior and Lord. We all thrive best through involvement in a faith community—the local church. Baptism into the faith, worship, and fellowship are important aspects of the choice to live as God's beloved.

Obstacles to Receiving Love

Clearly Scripture provides a starting foundation for God's love. But if this is true, why don't more women choose to see ourselves as deeply loved? One reason became quite clear to me a few years ago when I gave this assignment while speaking at a women's retreat. I had no idea it would end up being such a challenge:

Write a love letter from God to you.

What would He say if He were writing you today?

While I didn't actually plan to read their letters, I'd hoped it would be a great exercise for the attendees to better understand what we had been studying on God's everlasting love.

But that evening when I asked for a show of hands of those who had actually taken time to write such a letter, I was shocked to see only one person raise her hand. Several protested their excuses:

"Well it was hard to think of words of love God would say to me. All I kept hearing were words of indictment for all my failures."

"I started writing the love letter but I couldn't think of anything to say. Perhaps it's because I don't really feel loveable?"

"I know I could have put down some of the love passages from the Bible since they are God's words, but somehow I couldn't believe those words were actually meant for me."

How important it is to remind people that God's love for us is not based on what we've *done*, but who we *are*. His.

It's not deciding in my mind *I deserve to be loved*. Or manipulating my heart to feel loved. It's settling in my soul, *I was created by God, who formed me because He so much loved the very thought of me. When I was nothing, He saw something and declared it good. Very good. And very loved.* . . . God's love isn't based on me. It's simply placed on me. And it's the place from which I should live . . . loved.[3]

But I get it. My sisters' hesitancy. Their honesty, using words not all that foreign to my own experience. Because seeing myself as God's beloved has been a lifetime journey of fits and starts.

But one life experience helped me to make great strides. And, interestingly enough, it was duplicated by the one woman who raised her hand and shared about writing her love letter from God. She said, "At first it was hard for me to find the words, then I thought of my own daughter and how much I love her unconditionally. So I put myself in God's role as my Heavenly Father. When I began writing as though from a loving Father to His daughter, I couldn't stop. Even if my little girl yells at me or makes stupid decisions, my love for her does not change, though I am saddened. And I don't love her because she has always said and done just the right thing—she's not perfect. I love her because she's mine. I guess that's pretty much how God feels about me, you think?"

Yes, parental love can give us great understanding into the heart of God. Our children tend to bring out our deepest emotions of celebration, protection, fear, joy, frustration, gratitude, disappointment—all of which are encompassed in our love for them. A love many of us feel is endless and unconditional. (Even those who are not parents can understand this illustration as most of us have invested in the life and growth of another.)

But even our well-intentioned parental love pales in comparison to God's love for His children.

Because there are times with our children when our love *does* fail, we *do* let them down, we *aren't* there, or we offer advice instead of a listening ear. I believe most parents do the best they can with what they know while raising their children. Of course, sadly, some do not.

One of Jesus' biblical names is King of kings. Thus we His daughters are also royalty; we are heirs to all He has. And He owns it all. "God decided in advance to adopt us into his own family by bringing us to himself through Jesus Christ. This is what he wanted to do, and it gave him great pleasure" (Ephesians 1:5).

I first became a mother when I adopted three children ages nine, seven, and four (yes, all at the same time). So the whole concept of adoption rings true to me. Once they were not my own, but now they are. I would literally give anything I have (even my life) for these precious ones God has entrusted to me for thirty-six years. Unconditional love. Well at least as best I can in my own imperfect way.

> We are children, perhaps, at the very moment when we know that it is as children that God loves us—not because we have deserved his love and not in spite of our undeserving; not because we try and not because we recognize the futility of our trying; but simply because he has chosen to love us. We are children because he is our father; and all of our efforts, fruitful and fruitless, to do good, to speak truth, to understand, are the efforts of children, who, for all their precocity, are children still in that before we loved him, he loved us, as children, through Jesus Christ our Lord.[4]

Do you live as an adopted child of God, or do you still run around like an orphan—like it's all up to you and you have no Heavenly Father to provide and protect? Perhaps you had lousy examples of earthly parents and so are soured on the whole image. You may need to experience an inner healing in that area of your heart so you can receive the love God offers.

Romans 8:15 says, "You received God's Spirit when he adopted you as his own children. Now we call him, 'Abba, Father,'" meaning we can cry out to him, "Daddy!"

Now it's your turn. Write a letter from God to you today. If it helps to remember your own experience of parental love, let that guide you as you hear from your own Heavenly Father:

Dear _____ (your name),

_____

_____

_____

_____

_____

_____

_____

_____

_____

_____

_____

_____

_____

_____

_____

_____

_____

_____

_____

_____

_____

_____

Love always,
Your Heavenly Father

Searching for Love

Remember even those of us who had loving earthly fathers sometimes struggle to convince ourselves of such unconditional love. I was raised in a home where I was secure in my parents' love for me. Through both the love languages of encouraging words and acts of service, Mama and Daddy sought to give me a great foundation for life. And because they were also Christians, God was front and center of their value system.

But I still grew up with insecurities. The world can be cruel. Careless words thrown around on the playground like *bossy, chubby,* or even, *we don't want her on our team* began to erode any semblance of self-esteem at a young age. Because I knew in my heart that I actually *was* bossy (that's what girls wired for leadership are often called in childhood), I *was* chubby (lifelong struggle), and yes, I *was* a very inadequate athlete on the recess teams (see: *chubby*).

Later in high school I was a smart "good girl"—not a popular choice back in those days of 1960s free love. But I was always looking for love, and by that I meant a boyfriend who would understand me and feel the same way. Good luck with that! I never went to the prom and even decided to leave high school after my junior year. *Surely there were people somewhere who got my mix of interest in books, faith, music, and creativity?*

God graciously provided two important things when I arrived at Furman University in Greenville, South Carolina, at seventeen (a thousand miles from home where I knew not one soul). First He provided cool people who also loved the things I did and who sought to live out their faith. Second He deepened my commitment to Christ, not only as my Savior but finally as Lord of all in my life.

And so began the process of discovering who I was while simultaneously learning about the Christian life through an immersion in the Bible. The sheer number of verses on love staggered me!

But I still wanted *human* love—I just didn't know what I would have to do to get it. I dated some in college but mostly spent time with groups of friends. Several years out of college I first "fell in love." Sadly, he didn't love me with the same intensity—and so began my cycle into feeling unworthy. *What was wrong with me that I wasn't good enough for him?* Because he was a strong Christian man, I subconsciously began to try to jump through spiritual and moral hoops to prove I could be *the one* for him. All to no avail.

Unfortunately, even as I grew in my faith and commitment, I still fell for guys who seemed spiritually beyond me. At least that's why I thought they didn't choose me. Which did a number on my self-esteem. *Would I never be good enough for a Christian guy to love me?*[5]

Do you see where all this is leading? Into law and works and legalism. No one taught me that; I came up with it all on my own.

And that is how a strong Christian woman can accidentally miss the grace of God. Thinking that God's love is just like the human love that has been withheld because of one reason or another. Human love is often based on an effort to meet someone else's expectation. A love "as long as . . ." or "until . . ." But where's the security in that? No wonder love makes women (and men) crazy!

Think back over your own life and the human love you have sought and sometimes received. Perhaps it would be revealing to write down the name(s) and the takeaway(s) from that relationship.

Name	Kind of Love Received	How It Ended	My Takeaway

As you review your various human relationships, do you see how sometimes it is easy to project all your own baggage onto God? Your father was a strict disciplinarian, so God must always be reprimanding you. Your best friend was loyal until she met someone else who included her in a better clique, so God will probably move on to someone else too. That man loved you as long as you pleased him, but then you changed; surely God must be keeping score of your efforts to please as well.

Assurance of Love

We can't *be* perfect any more than we can *love* perfectly. However if we begin to live from a place of security, not striving, our relationships improve greatly. We are much less likely to demand from others what they simply cannot give—perfect love, purpose for life, absolute security. And we are more likely to be filled with gratitude and grace, thus pouring out to others in redemptive and restorative ways.

We will focus on how to live from a grace place in chapter seven. For now let me just say that seeking to earn love sent me into a spiral of self-recrimination and depression.

God's grace is what rescued me from a pattern of needing to be loved by someone in order to feel worthy as a person. But much more importantly, grace rescued me from the bondage of striving to *earn* God's love. I was released from being a POW (prisoner of works).

And now I live loved.

Love bade me welcome; yet my soul drew back,
      Guilty of dust and sin.
But quick-eyed Love, observing me grow slack
      From my first entrance in,
Drew nearer to me; sweetly questioning,
      If I lacked any thing.

"A guest," I answered, "worthy to be here—"
      Love said—"You shall be he."
"I, the unkind, ungrateful? Ah, my dear,
      I cannot look on thee."
Love took my hand; and smiling, did reply,
      "Who made the eyes, but I?"

> "Truth, Lord; but I have marred them; let my shame
>   Go where it doth deserve."
> "And know you not," says Love, "who bore the blame?"
>   "My dear, then I will serve."
> "You must sit down," says Love, "and taste my meat."
>   So I did sit and eat.
>
>   – George Herbert, "Love"[6]

Friend, we have been invited to sit and eat at the banquet solely because we are loved that much!

> Our identity is rooted in God's unconditional love for us. He has given us gifts and resources to make a unique contribution to the world for his glory. We work in partnership with him as we receive with a grateful heart the gifts he has given us, develop them and use them to contribute positively to this world. We honor him as we become all he created us to be, reaching out in love and service to our physical family, our spiritual family and community, and the larger human family to which we belong.[7]

When we are loved by someone, we draw close and stay near. We feel safe and secure, protected and cherished. Is this your experience in the presence of Jesus, who invites you and me to abide always in Him (John 15)? Read over these two passages from John, and write down your own reflections:

> "Very truly I tell you, one of you is going to betray me." His disciples stared at one another, at a loss to know which of them he meant. One of them, the disciple whom Jesus loved, was reclining next to him. Simon Peter motioned to this disciple and said, "Ask him which one he means." Leaning back against Jesus, he asked him, "Lord, who is it?"
>
>   —John 13:21–25 NIV

In His most trying hour in the upper room, Jesus revealed to His friends that one of them would betray Him. The passage says, "The disciple whom Jesus loved, was reclining next to him" and "leaning back against Jesus." Most scholars agree this disciple is John, son of Zebedee, his closest and truest friend. What would it take for you to picture yourself *that close* to Jesus? Are there ways you can better dwell in His constant presence and draw near?

_____

_____

_____

_____

_____

> No one has ever seen God. But the unique One, who is himself God, is near to the Father's heart. He has revealed God to us.
>
> —John 1:18

The Gospel of John tells us about Jesus—the unique One—as being "near to the Father's heart." How important is it for us to stay near to our Heavenly Father's heart? To be quiet enough to hear His very whisper? Just as John emulated the closeness Jesus had with the Father, what steps could you take to live as one who is truly loved?

_____

_____

_____

_____

_____

_____

What Does It Look Like When I Live Loved?

Because I am already loved and accepted, I need no longer find my worth through the response of others. Audiences, readers, family, friends, and even faith communities all have an opinion of me and how I answer God's call for my life. When that feedback is positive, I feel affirmed and validated. When it is negative, I too often feel crushed and discouraged. No more. Yes, I will pray for wisdom to learn from authentic, helpful criticism, but I will only allow myself to heed the audience of One.

Because I know the source of life and love, I intentionally choose to dwell constantly in God's presence. This means daily prayers and time in God's Word—making deposits into my soul that will reap benefits of God's peace, power, and provision as each new day unfolds. Thus I am filled with gratitude.

My never-changing identity is God's beloved. Everything else in my life may change. My status may change from single to married, then again to divorced or widowed. My vocation may consist of many and varied titles and jobs. One day I may be a mother, and tragically the next day I may lose my child. One day I may be loved by a man who says he would give his all for me. But he doesn't. One day I may be healthy and the next fighting a disease. Yet through it all, as I name Jesus Christ as my Lord and Savior, I am and will forever always be truly His beloved.

From my position as a receiver of unconditional love and the undeserved gift of grace, I commit my life to becoming a channel of both love and grace to others. I pray to see beyond the defensiveness and pain that so often spills out in anger or fear. Instead of a hurried and driven person, I become one who makes time to offer kindness, grace, and a listening ear.

No matter what happens in my life, I live as a person of faith who knows how the story ends—God wins. And when my life on earth is finished, I rest in the assurance that I will see Jesus face to face. I also live each day in the way I want to be remembered and trust that my own story and legacy has made a difference in someone's life. And for the kingdom.

O God of love, we pray Thee give us love;

Love in our thinking, love in our speaking,

Love in our doing, and love in the hidden places of our souls;

Love of our neighbours near and far;

Love of our friends, old and new;

Love of those with whom we find it hard to bear,

And love of those who find it hard to bear with us;

Love of those with whom we work,

And love of those with whom we take our ease;

Love in Joy, love in sorrow;

Love in life and love in death;

That so at length we may be worthy to dwell with Thee,

Who art eternal love.

—William Temple[8]

Becoming Soul Strong

What would it mean for you to daily see yourself as God sees you? As you think and pray about it, begin to write down some of your own goals as someone who is beloved. Imagine the unfolding of your life as a *soul strong* woman in the days ahead.

What might it look like for me to live loved?

_____

_____

_____

_____

_____

_____

_____

Chapter 2

Be Authentic

I discover and embrace my unique calling.

hemotherapy had not diminished her humor. Nor her wisdom. As she sat on the stage and regaled us with encouragement to write our stories with passion and purpose, I listened in the back of the auditorium utterly grateful for this human—cancer survivor, God's servant, and, yes, my friend, Liz Curtis Higgs.

"Don't worry so much about platform. Be who God created you to be and share your own unique message. All the rest is secondary. Remember the one thing that matters is Jesus!" And then, as though to emphasize what it means to be an authentic witness, she did the most remarkable thing ever.

She pulled off her wig, beamed in her baldness, and exclaimed, "Jesus is all that truly matters!"

The sound of silence filled the room. But only for a brief moment until the loud cheers and praises thundered.

I may not be brave enough to be that authentic. The very thought of it conjures up visions of walking naked in a crowd. But even so, that doesn't mean I'm inauthentic; I'm just on a journey toward more truth and transparency.

Back when I was growing up in a genteel Southern town, I didn't realize that each time I responded, "Everything is just fine," to someone's "How are you?" I was putting on a mask to hide pain, loneliness, or something complicated in my home or heart. It just seemed simpler and more acceptable to present that I've-got-it-all-together persona to everyone. After all, there was a lot at stake in admitting imperfection—not the least of which was my Christian witness.

Funny that. I don't think Jesus would have been embarrassed by my tarnished, crooked crown. After all, weren't His best friends a ragtag group of redeemed sinners? What Christ wants is a heart fully devoted to Him and an honest life reflecting His power in our humanity. Of course we stumble and fall. Yes, we have impossible assignments on terrible, horrible, no-good, very bad days. But how do we *respond* or *react* to such challenges in real life?

I wish now that I had felt free in my youth to answer those "How are you?" questions honestly. Something like, "Thanks for asking. I'm struggling with a few things right now but learning a lot in the process," or "Well most of the time things are going well, but today I just happen to be a bit discouraged," or even, "Honestly? I am feeling a bit alienated from my friends right now but trying to work it out." I guess I'll always wonder what their response might have been.

Fast forward to today. If anything, on the surface our culture now embraces imperfection. At least when it chooses. So instead of hiding our struggling selves we regurgitate them all over the world—through whatever platform we have. There is even a new term to describe this—*curated imperfection.* It seems to have begun with mommy bloggers acting real and evolved into a whole new skill set. But, as one woman observed, "The problem with . . . 'curated imperfection' is just that: it's staged. For every picture of a 'frazzled' mom with a large following cradling a cup of coffee in a [perfectly] messy bun, there's likely 20 others on her camera roll that didn't make the cut for Instagram."[1]

Thus the struggle—how do we live authentically without falling into the trap of "Everything's just fine" or the other end of "I'm a hot mess"? Surely there is some happy medium.

We do real. Authenticity is the quality of being genuine; real—one's true nature or beliefs. And I do believe most women today sincerely desire to live authentically.

> [Authenticity is] the clearing away of all that is not true, peeling back the layers until you discover what was there in the beginning. It's allowing yourself to be truly known and loved, as well as really knowing and loving someone else. It is the willingness to stand alone in doing what you believe is right, even when what's right isn't a popular choice. Authenticity can't be copied. . . . It resists comparison. It defies seeing yourself as who you are less than or who you're not. It's acknowledging the difference between what is fake and what is real. —*Magnolia Journal*, Spring 2019

When Liz Curtis Higgs took off her wig to reveal baldness from cancer chemotherapy, it was as though she was saying, *Yes, I'm a strong woman, but I'm also sick. And yes, I'm still speaking from the platform (although sitting in a chair, not standing at a podium) telling you an important true message that Jesus is all that truly matters.* Her authenticity was a tool to point others (we the audience) to where help and hope lay—in the power of Jesus Christ. It was clearly all about Him, not her.

We do real. But not so that others will be enthralled by our messy lives in order to justify their own. We do real so that others will see the God who is there for us in the midst of those fears, failures, and faith-challenges.

It's hard but necessary work to discover who we are and why we're here. But I believe that the heart of the spiritual journey is a willingness to recognize ourselves as we are in front of our Maker. Where are you on that journey? Many of us stay busy in order to avoid facing some of the deepest questions in our souls. But then we fail to understand both who we are and the work God has for us in the world. Why can't it be as simple as doing what Dolly Parton says, "Find out who you are. And do it on purpose"?

A *soul strong* woman seeks to be authentic. Embracing the following four truths can certainly contribute to this process:

I know who I am and who I'm not. I am confident in how God created me uniquely with gifts that serve His purpose for my life.

I live for an audience of One. While others' opinions do matter, I do and say all to the glory of God.

I reject comparison and competition. These temptations can negatively impact my calling to fulfill my part in the body of Christ.

I passionately pursue my calling. I learn to focus on both my primary calling in life as well as how each season manifests the "next things."

I Know Who I Am and Who I'm Not

David was the youngest son and a shepherd boy. His early life was spent alone in Bethlehem's hills and meadows, immersed in God's vast beauty and nature's might. As a result he became a worshipper and a poet. And occasionally, in order to protect his sheep, he had to battle lions and bears. Throughout this lonely season, God was drawing David close and giving him strength, courage, and a total dependence on the One whose presence he experienced.

So on that day David appeared at the battlefront to give his soldier brothers some food, his first thought upon hearing the taunts from the giant Goliath and seeing the intimidation of the Israelites was that this battle belonged to the Lord. How could others not see the power available in that? Armed with such courage and confidence he stepped forward and offered to fight the Philistine giant.

He received a mixed response—ridicule from his own family but an eventual support from his king. Because King Saul cared for this young man and also wanted victory, he insisted David put on his own armor—glistening metal and sharp sword. After all, this was the kind of warrior and leader the world seems to prefer—the flashy and fabulous. But David knew his personal expertise lay in the simple and strategic—five stones and a slingshot.

> David removed the helmet, unbelted the sword, and took off the armor. It couldn't have been easy to do that: walk away from all that proffered expertise. But to have gone to meet Goliath wearing Saul's armor would have been a disaster. Borrowed armor always is. David needed what was authentic to him.[2]

Before facing Goliath, David knelt at a stream, carefully selecting his ammunition, and, "He picked up five smooth stones from a stream and put them into his shepherd's bag" (1 Samuel 17:40). Eugene Petersen says this gesture frames something essential for each of us: "Are we going to live this life from our knees, imaginatively and personally? Or are we going to live it conventionally and at secondhand? Are we going to live out of our God-created, Spirit-anointed, Jesus-saved being?"[3]

When Goliath faced a small boy with a slingshot and a few stones, his moments were already numbered. Young as he was, David was living from a source of strength, confident "this is the LORD's battle, and he will give you to us!" (v. 47).

Think of a confident woman you know who appears to be comfortable in her own skin. What do you most admire about her?

_____

_____

_____

_____

_____

How do you feel when you are around her?

_____

_____

_____

_____

_____

Chances are you also experience more peace and security because this woman's assurance and calm allows you to settle into your best self.

I expect we'd all love to be that kind of woman, possessing the courage to say to someone in authority, "No thanks, what you've suggested is not a good fit—I will use what God gave me instead."

Paul knew "It's in Christ that we find out who we are and what we are living for" (Ephesians 1:11 *The Message*). Our Creator, Sustainer, and Redeemer fashioned us uniquely and perfectly. "Long before we first heard of Christ and got our hopes up, he had his eye on us, had designs on us for glorious living, part of the overall purpose he is working out in everything and everyone" (vv. 11–12 *The Message*).

Consider what these verses in Ephesians 1 affirm about knowing who you are and who you aren't:

Who helps me discover who I am?

_____

_____

_____

_____

_____

When did He begin to create me uniquely?

_____

_____

_____

_____

_____

And what where those designs for?

_____

_____

_____

_____

_____

Have you identified the overall purpose He is working in you?

Sometimes we have tools available to help understand our authentic selves. During the 1980s I lived and worked in Silicon Valley, California. Even now it's hard to describe the energy and explosion I experienced in that place as I entered my thirties. I served on the pastoral staff team of a large church on the cutting edge of ministry. Always eager to learn new ways to interact, our staff took the Myers-Briggs Type Indicator personality inventory so we could share our results with our peers and understand one another better.

I discovered I was an ENFJ (extroversion, intuition, feeling, judging), one of the rarest combinations and same as my senior pastor.

> ENFJs are driven by several things. They are invigorated by social novelty and networking with people. They are also motivated by personal excellence and self-mastery, including the sense of validation that comes from being esteemed and admired by others. Lastly, and perhaps most importantly, they strive to quicken the personal growth of others, which, in turn, fortifies their sense of purpose and self-worth.[4]

Well that certainly explains a lot!

The next year I was given the opportunity to take the Johnson O'Connor aptitude test, which proclaimed I was off the charts for something called ideaphoria, whatever that means . . . probably that I never stop coming up with new ideas. It also indicated that I am a highly subjective person. At least those are the two results I remember, probably because they have kept cropping up ever since.

Some of my colleagues are now embracing the Enneagram. Author Alice Fryling explains:

> The Enneagram suggests that we all have been given a particular gift from God . . . goodness, love, effectiveness, creativity, wisdom, faithfulness, joy, power, and peace. As we live with the special gift we have been given, we bump into roadblocks: we cannot do this perfectly, others do not appreciate our gifts, and others have different gifts that may look better or worse in our own eyes. When these roadblocks

> appear, we desperately try to affirm ourselves by exaggerating our gifts. . . . One of the values of the Enneagram is that it not only identifies the compulsions of the false self, it also suggests the grace that invites us to return to the true self.[5]

Someone once said that you have determined your Enneagram correctly if you wince when you find out what number you are. Well that was certainly the case when I discovered I am an Enneagram three with a two wing—which is described as the *achiever* (with a *helper* wing). Wince. Though I might be somewhat embarrassed to see achieving as a primary characteristic, I choose to focus instead on the fact that my type clarifies my vantage point for viewing life. If I know that I have certain proclivities, then I can better avoid dangerous traps and also pursue important growth areas.

For example, Enneagram threes are encouraged to be truthful.

> Be honest with yourself and others about your genuine feelings and needs. Likewise, resist the temptation to impress others or inflate your importance. You will impress people more deeply by being authentic than by bragging about your successes or exaggerating your accomplishments.[6]

Now I understand why it was important for me to include authenticity as one of the seven sections of how women become *soul strong*!

Yes, use feedback from respected friends and colleagues, and use personality testing as a tool to help pinpoint strengths and weaknesses. But most of all use God's Word to solidify exactly who you are in Him.

Take some time to look up these key affirmations and jot down words and phrases that speak to who you are.

I am the salt of the earth. (Matthew 5:13)

_____

_____

_____

I am the light of the world. (Matthew 5:14)

_____

_____

_____

I am God's disciple-maker. (Matthew 28:19)

_____

_____

_____

I am Jesus' friend. (John 15:15)

_____

_____

_____

I am greatly loved. (Romans 5:8)

_____

_____

_____

I am God's messenger to the world. (Acts 1:8)

_____

_____

_____

I am a place where God's Spirit lives. (1 Corinthians 6:19)

_____

_____

_____

I am a new person with a new life. (2 Corinthians 5:17)

_____

_____

_____

I am God's child. (Galatians 3:26)

_____

_____

_____

I am spiritually alive. (Ephesians 2:5)

_____

_____

_____

I am God's incredible work of art. (Ephesians 2:10)

_____

_____

_____

I am created In God's likeness. (Ephesians 4:24)

_____

_____

_____

I am totally and completely forgiven. (1 John 1:9)

_____

_____

_____

Friend, we are fearfully and wonderfully made. And we are definitely multidimensional. That's why it's important to recognize both the light and shadow sides of our personalities and gifts. I'm an extrovert who craves regular periods of silence and contemplation. I love both writing and speaking, but maybe speaking just a pinch more since it involves interaction with people.

We must resist the urge to let anyone pigeonhole us into a label—whether that be a role at church or work or even your fashion style, as Jessica Honnegar, the founder of *Noonday*, shared.

Sometimes I think that all of us, deep down, must not believe that we can be more than one thing. Strong *and* sensitive. Vocal *and* respectful. Brave *and* scared. . . . The truth is, I am a good mom *and* I also work. . . . I am a fashion executive *and* I'm curvy. I am passionate about caring for the poor *and* I love having fun with style. I just don't fit into a neat little box. And surely neither do you.[7]

How marvelous it is, O Lord, that you contemplated each of us before we were made! How marvelous that you considered and created us, decreeing the very time and place that each of us should enter the world, to live out our own part of your grand story. . . . You have created each of us, O Lord, to bear your image in unique expression, reflecting a facet of your glory in a way that no other person in all of history will, so that by knowing one another we might also know you better. . . . Bless this your child in the year to come. May they know the comfort of your presence, the certainty of your purpose, and consolation of your love at work in their life. Grant them wisdom, maturity, vision, and passion in increasing measure, that they might be an instrument well-honed for the building of your kingdom. Bless them with loving family and enduring friendships, that they might make their journey ever surrounded by the steadying companionship of fellow pilgrims. May they invest their moments well in the coming year and in all years to follow . . . Amen.
—Douglas McKelvey, "A Liturgy for the Marking of Birthdays"[8]

I Live for an Audience of One

As a speaker I care deeply for my audience. With them in mind, I carefully tailor my presentation and then ask the Holy Spirit to help me deliver words in an encouraging and challenging manner that points others to God as the source of all hope.

Sadly, my "self" stumbles into the way occasionally, and the focus turns on me, not them. Though it's only natural to want a positive response, that desire amplifies when something throws us off our gait. Like that time I awakened in a lovely guest room by the sea, preparing to speak three times to a beautiful gathering of hundreds of women.

Until my front tooth broke in half. As I looked into the mirror at my now snaggle-toothed face, my first thoughts were all about me. How awful I looked. Could the tooth ever be fixed? And then, horror of horrors, I remembered a videographer had been hired to record the entire day. Of course.

I prayed. I wept. Then I asked God to help me get over myself and minister to these hungry women.

What did I do? I spent the whole conference wearing bright coral lipstick speaking and laughing and chatting with women, never once acknowledging the obvious wide gap in the middle of my face. I lived for an audience of One—the God who had called and equipped me for that very moment in time. Just as I was. Real. Authentic.

In the final moments of the event I challenged us all to make the choice for a life of adventure in the presence, power, and purpose of God. Just as I had to choose that very day between allowing vanity to sidetrack my mission or to move forward imperfectly with all I had to offer. I thanked the women for their grace and generosity, "My prayer is that when you too show up with nothing much but pure obedience, the world will listen and love you as well."

The next time something breaks in your life just as you are about to embark on kingdom work, will you choose to recognize it for what it is—a temptation to get sidetracked, rattled, or to give up? Don't do it. Because you and I are simply the vessels of the treasure deep inside. "We now have this light shining in our hearts, but we ourselves are like fragile clay jars containing this great treasure. This makes it clear that our great power is from God, not from ourselves" (2 Corinthians 4:7). When I live for an audience of One, my deepest desire is to glorify my most important audience—God.

Not that our listeners be spellbound. Not that our tribe be satisfied. Not that our social media reach be expanded. Not that our personality be embraced. We are not called to follow Christ, build the kingdom, and please people. Paul learned this the hard way. By accumulating the accolades (from people) he almost lost the Audience (of God).[9]

But grace changed all that. And Paul could never go back. "It is not clear to you that to go back to that old rule-keeping, peer-pleasing religion would be an abandonment of everything personal and free in my relationship with God? I refuse to do that, to repudiate God's grace" (Galatians 2:21 *The Message*).

Just as there are many voices competing for our attention, there are countless people and platforms who constantly (and usually without our invitation to do so) evaluate our work, our words, and our lives. Which feedback speaks the loudest and receives your full attention? That may actually depend on your story thus far. Whom have you allowed to shape and define you in the past?

Margot Starbuck has written and spoken extensively on how childhood rejections affected her own tendency to perform for the masses' approval. Now on the healthy side of finding her identity solely as God's beloved, she reflects on many who are still seeking. She writes, "We long to see the face that is truly gracious, the one that accepts us exactly as we are, but our vision has been distorted. Because our worth has been reflected to us through human faces—critical, disappointed, distracted, angry, sad, or even absent faces—we may have perceived that we weren't worthy of unconditional love and acceptance. And we fail to see the face that is true."[10]

Think back to the many faces you saw and voices you heard while growing up and consider how they may have affected the way you see yourself today:

When I think of my mother, I hear her saying this to me _____

_____

When I think of my father, I hear him saying this to me _____

_____

Teachers often referred to me as _____

_____

My childhood girlfriends thought of me as _____

_____

My first feedback from guys was that I was _____

_____

When the pastor spoke to me, he communicated _____

_____

My boss at my first job evaluated me as _____

_____ encouraged me in this

way _____

_____crushed my spirit in this way

_____

When I think of my husband, I hear him saying this to me _____

_____

I received the most encouragement from _____

in my younger life.

Now that you have identified some of the voices contributing to your thoughts about who you are, what can you do with that knowledge? Begin by taking it to the Lord in prayer. Pour out your heart and thank Him for the people who have encouraged you through the years, and ask Him to help you become willing to forgive those who hurt you.

Yes, asking God to bless that person who hurt you is challenging, even grueling, but the result is freedom. . . . It's hard to believe, but the one hurt the most by your resentment and continued bitterness is not the one who rejected you. It's you. . . . God has so much more for you than being stuck in the prison of unforgiveness.[11]

Be willing to seek professional counseling as needed, which can be an investment in your mental, emotional, spiritual, and physical health.

> We do not confront the past for the purpose of blaming others or making excuses for ourselves; we explore past experiences and messages to uncover the lies that are misleading us and to enter more fully into the truth. Only then can we be free from self-absorption and self-deprecation and give to God and others from the fullness he intends.[12]

Paul was clear on who his audience of one was—the Lord Himself. "As for me, it matters very little how I might be evaluated by you or by any human authority. . . . It is the Lord himself who will examine me and decide" (1 Corinthians 4:3–4). His all-important audience of one was the Lord.

What audience are you seeking?

What about Social Media?

The old phrase "keeping up with the Joneses" has a new meaning today. With the onslaught of social media, everyone has come face-to-face with the daily challenge of keeping up with everyone else. We all seem to need an audience. And the bigger the better. Social media has become a driving force for approval and endorsement. But think about who is behind all those likes—are they really the ones you seek to please?

Are you confident enough to live your unique life and calling in truth and freedom, regardless of numbers or feedback? All of us want to make a difference in the world and reach as many as possible with the hope we have discovered in Christ. But each of us must decide what that costs in terms of time, energy, and integrity.

Social media is a fabulous way to stay connected to friends and family, to learn from those we might never have met before, and to share the creative side of life. But this technological tool can also turn into a temptation—when it slowly becomes our alternative reality without any accountability. Home décor maven Joanna Gaines, who has a huge public platform, warns, "What [social media] shouldn't be is a means to measure our worth or compare our lot in life with another's. It is not an honest mirror or window, because that view is always obscured to the point of only catching a glimpse. Don't fall for the trap and believe it's anything more than a snapshot in time, even it's highly edited and beautifully presented."[13]

A snapshot in time. Not the whole story or the whole picture of our lives, just a glimpse. And yet those glimpses can be used by God to lift a spirit, prod a memory, teach a life lesson, or comfort a soul. And well we know that it only takes a glimpse to also crush a spirit, fuel a fire, judge a fellow human, and shame a sinner. Which would you like your posts to accomplish during that quick scroll by someone else's fingers?

Is it even possible to be authentic on social media without going to either extreme—airbrushed perfection or curated imperfection? I find that answering the following six questions helps me in deciding on what I will throw out there into the world wide web:

1. *What is my motive in posting this?*

   Am I bragging, sharing something best kept quiet, or provoking controversy?

2. *Is the content rooted in truth and my values?*

   Am I sharing fake news, a false image of my life, or something that could reflect negatively on someone else?

3. *Is this post helpful?*

   Does it celebrate, encourage, offer hope, give positive information, or even share humor (at no one's expense)?

4. *Could this post be hurtful or harmful?*

   Am I betraying a trust, sharing someone else's news too soon, revealing family secrets, potentially endangering a child, or disobeying employee social rules?

5. *Will I cringe when this post pops up next month or next year?*

   What would my future self say about what I'm considering making public today?

6. *Does this post give glory to God?*

   Does my social media witness as a Christ follower draw others to Him and His people?

When we meet Jesus face-to-face I don't think He is going to ask us how successful we were in the eyes of culture. Instead perhaps God will ask us to reflect on the nature of our relationship with Him. One pastor imagines such questions as

Did you do My will?

Did you live the life I created you to live?

Did you become the person I created you to be?

Did you live a life of love with Me and all that I created?[14]

Will we be able to echo Jesus who prayed in the Garden of Gethsemane, "I have brought you glory on earth by finishing the work you gave me to do" (John 17:4 NIV). We bring God glory when all we do points to Him and not us.

I Reject Comparison and Competition

Several years ago I was a returning faculty at a writers' conference and was approached by a young woman who thanked me for my classes the previous year. She proceeded to list all my suggestions she had implemented since then into her writing and speaking ministry, which was by all appearances thriving.

I was so gratified to hear this fruit, as you can imagine.

That is until she contacted me about six months later with the amazing news she had landed a multiple book contract with a major publisher and wanted to know if I would consider endorsing her first book. Now let me explain where I was when all this happened. That very week I had two different book proposals rejected from that very same publisher, one with whom I had a great working relationship. Frankly, news of this other writer's success stung.

But my immediate response to this budding author? Of course I was thrilled with her contracts and would most definitely read her first book and send in an endorsement. I said those words, and I meant them sincerely. With all my heart.

Well, at least until I hung up the telephone. And the green-eyed monster appeared: *Can you believe it? They turned you down and went with an unknown first-timer? Maybe you need to just face the reality that you are washed-up and irrelevant. You have nothing left to say and no one to listen. Time to throw in the towel, girlie!* Hiss. Hiss.

Every time we compare ourselves with someone else, we are in danger of believing the lie of rejection—that our own life is not important. I am so ashamed to confess to you that it took me more than a moment to close my ears and holler, "In the name of Jesus, begone with your lies!"

As I write, it all sounds so utterly ridiculous. Did I mention this very talented and smart young woman writes and speaks in a totally different genre and platform? We are partners in ministry, not competitors!

What made me immediately jump to comparing and self-condemnation? Temporarily forgetting who I am in Christ and what He has called me to do. Whenever that happens, a door cracks open, allowing insecurity and envy to sneak inside.

Too often we want what someone else appears to have. Perhaps we even idolize who they are. Timothy Keller says, "An idol is whatever you look at and say, in your heart of hearts, 'If I have that, then I'll feel my life has meaning, then I'll know I have value, then I'll feel significant and secure.'"[15]

But we don't, do we? We never quite have enough, and then our relationships get sticky. Emily P. Freeman, in her book *The Next Right Thing*, wonders, "When we are comparing, we cannot connect. It's just not possible. To some degree, we all question where we fit and how we're perceived. . . . Could it be possible that the person you're competing with most is some idealized version of yourself that you can never live up to?"[16]

What shall we do when we face competition from both without and within? My own strategy when such times come is to remind myself that I am loved and chosen by God, to take one step toward obeying what He has called me to do that day, and finally to make a deliberate choice to promote and lift up that other person.

This is nothing new, as Paul addressed such things in the early church. "Isn't everything you have and everything you are sheer gifts from God? So what's the point in all this comparing and competing—you already have all you need" (1 Corinthians 4:7 *The Message*).

We were created, redeemed, and sustained in order to live our unique story—yes, with all the mess, mistakes, meanderings, and even miracles.

Those who need to know us will be put in our path by a sovereign God. You were not created to be her. Isn't that a relief?

In the following verse Peter—who certainly walked a rocky road to authentic living—strongly admonishes us to recognize that God gives all we need. As you read, make this promise personal to your own life:

> By his divine power, God has given us everything we need for living a godly life. We have received all of this by coming to know him, the one who called us to himself by means of his marvelous glory and excellence.

—2 Peter 1:3

What has God given me?

_____

_____

_____

What did I do to receive this?

_____

_____

_____

What action has He taken toward me?

_____

_____

_____

Do you believe we truly have been given everything we need? Or are you grasping to take hold of that which has been given to your sister? Even though in God's sovereignty and wisdom, He has chosen not to give you *her* house, *her* clients, *her* friends, or *her* platform at this time.

Her success does not mean your failure.

Lord Jesus, we are silly sheep who have dared to stand before You and try to bribe You with our preposterous portfolios. Suddenly we have come to our senses. We are sorry and ask You to forgive us. Give us the grace to admit we are ragamuffins, to embrace our brokenness, to celebrate Your mercy when we are at our weakest, to rely on Your mercy no matter what we may do. Dear Jesus, gift us to stop grandstanding and trying to get attention, to do the truth quietly without display, to let the dishonesties in our lives fade away, to accept our limitations, to cling to the gospel of grace, and to delight in Your love. Amen.
—Brennan Manning[17]

I Passionately Pursue My Calling

Frederick Buechner once said, "The place God calls you to is the place where your deep gladness and the world's deep hunger meet."

Of course there is a universal calling for every believer. Fuller Theological Seminary president Mark Labberton defines this universal calling as, "To live as a follower of Jesus today. In every aspect of life, in small and large acts, with family, neighbors and enemies, we are to seek to live out the grace and truth of Jesus. This is our . . . calling."[18] He calls this primary statement "first things." How this is manifested in the varying details and seasons of life is secondary—"next things." Although these specific job titles matter, they are not our primary calling.

My primary calling is to live as Christ's beloved.

As I live into this primary calling—my first thing—I am empowered also to love God and my neighbor through various marching orders and job titles—those next things.

Scripture clearly outlines the call of each person who is a follower of Christ. Look up each verse and write next to it your firm calling:

Romans 1:6

I am called to _____

1 Corinthians 1:9

I am called to be in _____

Colossians 3:15

I am called to _____

2 Corinthians 5:17–20

I am called to _____

Galatians 5:13

I am called to be _____

2 Timothy 1:9

I am called to be _____

1 John 3:1

I am called a _____ [19]

Every believer is called to the above. Which ones do you find the hardest to live into?

_____

_____

_____

_____

_____

But how do you discern your unique calling?

_____

_____

_____

_____

_____

My first job out of Furman University at the ripe age of twenty-one was as an editor for a small magazine, *Carolina Country.* I loved words. I loved creating. And, after all, I now had a bright shiny Bachelor of English degree under my belt. So I moved to Raleigh, North Carolina, and began to immerse myself in journalism. I soon discovered that while I was learning so much about writing, editing, and publishing, there was a whole part of my heart that wasn't being utilized very much in my vocation—compassionate outreach to needy people.

So because I was very young and still trying on hats—I did a vocational one-eighty-degree turn and got a job for the North Carolina Department of Services for the Blind (as it was called back then) as an orientation and mobility teacher for the twenty western counties of North Carolina. I traveled all the back-road hills and worked with visually impaired children and adults, teaching them how to thrive in the midst of their disability. This was hard work, but it fed my soul every time one of my clients made a breakthrough toward independence or hope.

In the midst of struggling with the dichotomy of wanting to write and wanting to make a difference in people's lives, I ended up saying yes to being a chaperone on a bus of college students headed to InterVarsity's Urbana Missions Conference. That one little yes opened my eyes and heart to a whole new world as I sat under the daily teaching of John Stott, Elisabeth Elliot, Helen Roseveare, Festo Kivengere, Billy Graham, and Luis Palau. It was there I prayed a prayer, "Lord, I will go anywhere and do anything for You!" (My simple version of John Wesley's covenant prayer.)

Who knew the first place He'd send me was seminary in Boston? After all this was the 1970s, and I honestly didn't even realize women could go to seminary. But I knew that whatever my future held, I wanted to be prepared with solid biblical and theological knowledge. After earning my master's degree at Gordon-Conwell Theological Seminary and studying communications at Wheaton College Graduate School, I then began a lifetime vocational journey combining both communication and compassion.

Along the way wise and godly people spoke into my life, recognized gifts, or made suggestions on discernment. As a seminarian I lived with widowed Elisabeth Elliot and helped type her manuscripts and drive her to speaking events. I was only twenty-five when she said to me, "Cindy, God has given you the ability to write, and it is your duty to write for Him."

Leighton Ford was at the helm of the Lausanne Committee for World Evangelization, where I worked as an editor my first job out of seminary. In his book *Survival Guide for the Soul*, pastor Ken Shigematsu shares the wise words Leighton Ford gave to him and which are helpful to anyone making an important life decision, "If you have reflected on what choice to make and have prayed about it, but don't discern any clear 'answer' from God, then try to project where you most want to be at the end of your life and go through the door you want to go through and trust God to make it right."[20] When perplexed between two opportunities, I envision choosing one and how that might unfold in all the areas of my life. Often there is an accompanying confirmation or check in my spirit.

Choose the path that appears to coincide with the arc of your life. I believe choices are so important I wrote a companion book to this one to encourage the practice of daily wise choices called, *Life-Giving Choices: 60 Days to What Matters Most.* It is actually within our power to decide each day *how* we will live out the numerous interruptions, joys, crises, and surprises that come our way as twenty-first century women. With endless resources provided by the One who knows us best and loves us most—God, the creator and sustainer of the universe.

The great news is God is not limited by our decisions—He can confirm a call, redirect us, or even open a surprising new door of opportunity. Our greatest choice is obedience to His will and His way. But that looks different on each person.

God's call can look like being a missionary or an evangelist for a living or it can be linked to your profession, your athletic ability, your vocational training, your love for math and science, your desire to write or create. The Lord can use anything—your talents, your expertise, your gifts, your interests, your past life experience—to draw you towards how and where He wants to use you as a person of influence. . . . God promises to not only call and involve us, but to equip us to be able to do what He asks us to do. . . . And, oftentimes, He asks us to take a baby step forward—to commit to something small first. He will provide the power and the wisdom and the sustenance. The Lord does not leave us on our own.[21]

I love how Moses's story so clearly illustrates these principles. He certainly had a rich background filled with seemingly opposing roles—prince of Egypt and murderer, a solitary life on the family farm and a public life leading an entire nation. There were for Moses—as there inevitably are for us—times of drawing closer to God in the wilderness and times of boldly going forth to fulfill our destiny.

Perhaps my favorite conversation is when God asks Moses to do something he feels totally unqualified to do. In Exodus chapter 3 we find Moses going about his business tending sheep when the voice of the Lord called his name, "Moses! Moses!" (v. 4).

God had been grooming Moses for that very moment as He revealed both the need and the call: "I have certainly seen the oppression of my people in Egypt. I have heard their cries of distress because of their harsh slave drivers. Yes, I am aware of their suffering. . . . Now go, for I am sending you to Pharaoh. You must lead my people Israel out of Egypt" (vv. 7, 10).

Record Moses's responses:

God says: "You must lead my people Israel out of Egypt" (v. 10).

Moses responds: _____

_____ (v. 11)

God says: "I will be with you" (v. 12).

Moses protests: _____

_____ (v. 13)

God says: "Say this to the people of Israel: I AM has sent me to you" (v. 14).

Moses protests again: _____

_____ (4:1)

God says: "If they do not believe you and are not convinced by the first miraculous sign, they will be convinced by the second sign" (v. 8).

But Moses pleaded: _____

_____ (v. 10)

God says: "Now go! I will be with you as you speak, and I will instruct you in what to say" (v. 12).

But Moses again pleaded: _____ (v. 13)[22]

> Moses wasn't qualified . . . [He] was past middle age when God called him to lead his children out of Egypt, and he spoke with a stutter. He was reluctant and unwilling and he couldn't control his temper. But he saw the bush that burned and was not consumed. He spoke with God in the cloud on Mount Sinai, and afterwards his face glowed with such brilliant light that the people could not bear to look at him.[23]

Do you ever find yourself arguing with God about an assignment?

I will never forget when it became abundantly clear to me that my life story would include marrying a widower and adopting three children ages nine, seven, and four—all at the same time! I assure you my Moses-like response to God was something like, "How can I possibly be the wife and mother these precious people need?" God's assurance of "I will be with you and give you what you need" gave me courage to do just that. For the past thirty-six years.

At the start of my marriage, Madeleine L'Engle's book *Walking on Water* fed my soul. Even today I can recite her words by heart because they were used to help make me *soul strong* back then.

> We are all asked to do more than we can do. Every hero and heroine of the Bible does more than he would have thought it possible to do, from Gideon to Esther to Mary. . . . In a very real sense not one of us is qualified, but it seems that God continually chooses the most unqualified to do his work, to bear his glory. If we are qualified, we tend to think that we have done the job ourselves. If we are forced to accept our evident lack of qualification, then there's no danger that we will confuse God's work with our own, or God's glory with our own.[24]

God will fill in all our gaps. But we have strengths too! Write down some things you love doing or things you do very well (as Frederick Buechner calls it, "your deep gladness"):

1.

2.

3.

List the talents and skills you possess that might be involved in the above activities:

_____

_____

_____

Now pray for the weaving together of all things by a Sovereign God. My perennial favorite prayer for direction is a Puritan prayer adapted by John Wesley.

> I am no longer my own, but Thine.
> Put me to what Thou wilt, rank me with whom Thou wilt.
> Put me to doing, put me to suffering.
> Let me be employed for Thee or laid aside for Thee,
> exalted for Thee or brought low for Thee.
> Let me be full, let me be empty.
> Let me have all things, let me have nothing.
> I freely and heartily yield all things to Thy pleasure and disposal.
> And now, O glorious and blessed God, Father, Son and Holy Spirit,
> Thou art mine, and I am Thine.
> So be it.
> And the Covenant, which I have made on earth,
> Let it be ratified in heaven. Amen.[25]

Becoming Soul Strong

Most of us are very good at wearing masks and hiding our true selves. In an effort to become more authentic, take some time to reflect on how you could begin removing your own mask—that false self you occasionally present to the world.

How do you think people describe you?

_____

_____

_____

How do you wish people would describe you?

_____

_____

_____

What parts of your self are you hiding?

_____

_____

_____

What is your deep passion—that which compels you?

_____

_____

_____

What is something most people don't know about you?

_____

_____

_____

What do you try to portray in front of others?

_____

_____

_____

What is really true about yourself that you wish others knew?

_____

_____

_____

What happens when you talk and act in an authentic manner?

_____

_____

_____

How can you let go of fear of what others might think of the real you?

_____

_____

_____

How could you live today so that your public actions reflect your own values and vision for your life? What would this look like?

_____

_____

_____

Chapter 3

Dwell Deep

I abide daily in God's presence, nourishing my soul.

o you ever just want *more*? More peace. More purpose. More power. Your desire is calling you deeper. Not to just know all *about* God but to know Him intimately. That desire from within is a hunger for more of God. The Almighty. The King of kings and Lord of lords. Creator and sustainer of the universe. The one who spun the stars into space and counts every hair on your head. The Man of Sorrows who sends the Comforter.

The great I Am wants more of you too. The Bread of Life is here to feed you. The Living Water is eager to quench your thirst. The Light of the World longs to shine your path, revealing His way. Can you even imagine such a thing?

> No eye has seen, no ear has heard, and no mind has imagined what God has prepared for those who love him.
>
> —1 Corinthians 2:9

Your desire for more of God than you have right now, your longing for love, your need for deeper levels of spiritual transformation than you have experienced so far is the truest thing about you. You might think that your woundedness or your sinfulness is the truest thing about you

> or that your giftedness or your personality type or your job title or your identity as husband or wife, mother or father, somehow defines you. But in reality, it is your desire for God and your capacity to reach for more of God than you have right now that is the deepest essence of who you are. . . . From this place we *cry out to God* for deeper union with Him and with others.[1] (emphasis added)

Beyond all imagination we are loved and invited into love. Hear Jesus as He longs to keep company with you: "Are you tired? Worn out? Burned out on religion? Come to me. Get away with me and you'll recover your life. I'll show you how to take a real rest. Walk with me and work with me—watch how I do it. Learn the unforced rhythms of grace. I won't lay anything heavy or ill-fitting on you. Keep company with me and you'll learn to live freely and lightly" (Matthew 11:28–30 *The Message*).

Will you go to Him and let Him teach you? Why not begin by recognizing your own desire?

Sit quietly for a moment and ask God to reveal the deepest desire of your heart. Jesus once asked blind Bartimaeus, "What do you want me to do for you?" (Mark 10:51). Restoring his sight seemed like the apparent answer, but Jesus forced Bartimaeus to put his desires into words and a plea, "My Rabbi . . . I want to see!" (v. 51).

Jesus asks you today, "What do you want Me to do for you?" What is your answer?

_____

_____

_____

_____

_____

_____

If part of your answer was like part of mine, then you are desperate to dwell in a deep and intimate relationship with the one who knows you best and loves you most. But there is partnership in pursuing such a life-giving journey. Ruth Haley Barton points out that "Our part is to offer ourselves lovingly and obediently to God. God's part is to work within us and our desires doing what He alone can do." She suggests a way to begin:

> We bring our ache for change, our longing for belonging, our desperation to make a difference. Then we keep company with Jesus by making space for him through a spiritual discipline. . . . But unless we open ourselves to him through spiritual practices, we will miss his coming altogether.[2]

This is what the LORD says: "Stop at the crossroads and look around. Ask for the old, godly way, and walk in it. Travel its path, and you will find rest for your souls."

—Jeremiah 6:16

A lot of people want to be spiritual. But the truth is most people don't want it enough to do what it takes to be godly, wise, and, yes, holy. We cannot know God and live the life He calls us to by simply having a *weekly* spiritual rhythm (church, a Bible study). We must spend time with Him in prayer, meditation on and study of His Word, and worship through a *daily* spiritual rhythm. What is that old, godly way in which Jeremiah encourages us to walk? It is the ancient practice of spiritual disciplines. And there truly is no other way. Trust me.

> We have to believe that the most significant opportunity before us every day is the opportunity to sit at the feet of Jesus. We won't rearrange our priorities until we really believe this is the best one.[3]

When It All Changed

I don't remember exactly when it happened, but there was a seismic shift when my morning prayers went from being merely a spiritual activity to check off my daily to-do list and transformed into my most important priority for embracing life each day.

I had finally grasped the truth in both my mind and heart—without daily prayer and time in God's Word we simply cannot live as *soul strong* followers of Christ. It's that simple.

Of course *we* make spiritual life complicated by coming up with all sorts of strategies for devotions, prayer books with multiple ribbons, and accompanying guilt every time we miss the mark. *Oh no—I neglected daily prayer three mornings in a row! Should I start all over again or just give up?*

Saint Benedict offered the sage advice, "Always we begin again." Because there is grace on the path toward sanctification.

When I was a college student we were taught to have a quiet time, preferably in the mornings. It was a good discipline for a new believer, and I was determined to include this practice in my growing repertoire of spiritual disciplines. I began keeping prayer journals, recording my petitions and answers to prayer. I purchased many, many devotional books and diligently read the entries, catching up whenever I missed a day. I enrolled in a small group Bible study and began to read through Scripture, learning more than I ever dreamed about God, Jesus, and the Holy Spirit. I loved how the stories in both Testaments came alive to me in a fresh way. I even learned acronyms to help keep me on track while I prayed, such as TRIP—thanksgiving, repentance, intercession, and petition. Later I discovered rich prayer books filled with ancient petitions that echoed my own heart's cry.

But it seemed I needed a monastic life in order to juggle all these practices with success. My own days were full and peppered with constant interruptions. Whether I was a studious graduate student, an overachieving young professional, a distracted new wife, an overwhelmed mama to four children, or busy author on a deadline, I struggled with keeping God first in my life.

Can you relate to the challenge of figuring out how to dwell deep? Do not allow shame or remorse to paralyze you.

It is not wrong to be tired. It is not wrong to feel overwhelmed. It's not wrong to go through seasons of complete chaos. What is wrong—and heartbreakingly foolish and wonderfully avoidable—is to live a life with more craziness than we want because we have less Jesus than we need.[4]

Lectio Divina

Lectio Divina ("divine reading") is one practice that may help open our hearts to what God is saying to us through His Word. When we study Scripture, we read seeking to understand its meaning. *Lectio Divina* is a way of studying Scripture by slowly reading one passage over and over again, listening for the impact of the words on our hearts. As we reflect on each word and phrase, it's almost as though we are praying the Scriptures. And, indeed, the Holy Spirit impresses a message upon us.

The first step is to decide on a portion of Scripture. Let's look at Isaiah 30:15–21 as we continue to seek ways to dwell deep. Following the Scripture is a list of eight suggested steps for practicing your own *Lectio Divina* with regard to any Scripture passage.

This is what the Sovereign LORD, the Holy One of Israel, says: "Only in returning to me and resting in me will you be saved. In quietness and confidence is your strength. But you would have none of it. You said, 'No, we will get our help from Egypt. They will give us swift horses for riding into battle.' But the only swiftness you are going to see is the swiftness of your enemies chasing you! One of them will chase a thousand of you. Five of them will make all of you flee. You will be left like a lonely flagpole on a hill or a tattered banner on a distant mountaintop." So the LORD must wait for you to come to him so he can show you his love and compassion. For the LORD is a faithful God. Blessed are those who wait for his help. O people of Zion, who live in Jerusalem, you will weep no more. He will be gracious if you ask for help. He will surely respond to the sound of your cries. Though the Lord gave you adversity for food and suffering for drink, he will still be with you to teach you. You will see your teacher with your own eyes. Your own ears will hear him. Right behind you a voice will say, "This is the way you should go," whether to the right or to the left.

Guidelines for *Lectio Divina*

Prepare: Before you read anything, quiet your heart, breathe deeply, and spend some time in silence.

First Reading: Read the Scripture slowly, pausing at each punctuation mark to breathe and let the words soak in. After this first reading, spend at least two minutes in silence.

Second Reading: As you slowly read the passage again, allow your pauses between phrases to be longer as you determine which words seem to be speaking directly to you. Take some time to write down thoughts, words, and phrases after you have finished this second reading.

Third Reading: In your third reading, be sure to stop when you come to one of those words or phrases that spoke to you earlier. Repeat each phrase in a prayerful way as you await God's whisper into your heart.

Ponder: As you continue to reflect on those special words, repeat them and prayerfully consider what God might be trying to say to you. Submit your thoughts, emotions, and complementary passages to filter through, noting what deep part of you is touched by these particular words.

Pray: Now it's time to actually ask God, "What would You say to me today through this verse?" Enter a season of silence as you listen to the Spirit. Begin to jot down any thoughts that come unbidden as you sense His presence.

Rest: Breathe deeply and settle comfortably in your seat as you embrace a season of silence for at least five minutes. Relish this time by simply basking in God's presence. You don't need to *do* anything at all. Just *be* in the moment.

Respond: As your time in this passage draws to a close, ask God, "As a result of these word gifts, what would You have me do?" He may be asking you to add to or remove something from your life. He may be calling you out to love and risk and sacrifice. Maybe you will change your attitude. Write out the assignment you believe He is giving you.

Close: Thank God for meeting you in this sacred place through His Word. As you leave the silence and reflection, be at peace.

Dwell

Today's good news is that Jesus, who loves us more than we can possibly imagine, knows our lives and gently beckons. "Dwell in Me, and I will dwell in you" (John 15:4 AMPC).

The word *dwell* usually conjures up one of the two most frequent definitions: where we live or where we focus. When Jesus calls us to dwell with Him, He is using the same word, which in Hebrew also means to nest. That's why the psalmist used bird imagery when he wrote about God covering him with feathers and offering secure refuge "under his wings" (Psalm 91:4 NIV).

Using that same imagery of eagles, those who are seeking to dwell deep might consider three aspects of that process: refuge, residency, and release. First God's unconditional love is a *refuge*. "How priceless is your unfailing love, O God! People take refuge in the shadow of your wings" (Psalm 36:7 NIV). Can't you just imagine an eaglet nestling into safety under its mother's wings?

Secondly we are told to make "the Most High your shelter" (Psalm 91:9 NLT). God doesn't want us to just visit Him. He wants us to make our hearts His home. If we will abide, He promises to reside. The word *shelter* in Psalm 91:9 is sometimes translated from the original Hebrew as residence, which is a period of advanced training. And that is just what we do each day as we pray and study the Bible.

Eagles and other predators are born with instincts that urge them to fly and pounce, but precisely *how* to do these things is another matter. In the life of a young eagle, both parents are always showing their offspring how to grow into the magnificent and powerful creature they are intended to become. Residency is a good time to learn how to incorporate spiritual disciplines into our everyday lives. We do what we observe our heavenly Father doing—eventually coming into our own.

But all this deep dwelling is for the greater purpose of *release*. We were not made to stay in the nest forever but to fly out into the world. "But those who trust in the LORD will find new strength. They will soar high on wings like eagles" (Isaiah 40:31). This period when baby eagles are urged by their parents to leave their nest is called fledging. The mother circles the nest with food, just out of reach, urging the eaglet to leave its aerie. Soon the eaglet is out seeking its own food and life. The eagle parents' duty was to birth the eaglets, raise them, teach them, and then release them out of their comfort zone.

As we continue to practice the presence of God, He releases us into the unknown. Whether it's a scary place or an exciting place, if we have spent time soaking up God's presence, peace, and power, we are ready to fly out into a broken world with the healing and hope-filled words of Christ![5]

There is no specific magic formula for spiritual growth, and so I'm not going to give you only one path to becoming and remaining *soul strong*. Though I am a firm believer that beginning each morning in silence, prayer, and Bible reading helps gird me for the day ahead, I realize this simply isn't possible for everyone. I also like to end my day with the prayer of Examen (we'll talk more about this prayer practice in the next chapter). Figure out what works for you. And once you've established a routine, be prepared for it to change as the seasons and responsibilities of your life change.

"Come near to God and he will come near to you" (James 4:8 NIV). Drawing near to Him is the first step, as this old hymn so beautifully reminds us:

There is a place of comfort sweet, near to the heart of God;

A place where we our Savior meet, near to the heart of God.

O Jesus, blest Redeemer, sent from the heart of God,

Hold us who wait before Thee near to the heart of God.

—Cleland Boyd McAfee, "Near to the Heart of God"

Rule of Life

> Keep your eyes open for GOD, watch for His works; be alert for signs of his presence. Remember the world of wonders he has made.

> —Psalm 105:4–5 *The Message*

Did you notice all the action words in this passage—*keep* your eyes open, *watch* for His works, *be alert* for signs of His presence, *remember* the world of wonders?

For me, this verse is a warning not to get complacent with life as I know it but rather to continually *engage* in my own sphere, actively seeking out what God is doing in the world. Easy to say; hard to do.

Without an intentional plan, I could easily squander my time and energies with no clear focus. That's one reason that a decade ago I began to embrace an ancient practice known as developing a Rule of Life. This time-honored practice has helped ordinary people live extraordinary and deepened spiritual lives through a personal living covenant with God. Living intentionally comes from my desire to integrate both my daily life experiences and my spiritual life through spiritual disciplines.

Pastor Peter Scazzero says a Rule of Life is an "intentional, conscious plan to keep God at the center of everything we do. It provides guidelines to help us continually remember God as the Source of our lives. It includes our unique combination of spiritual practices that provide structure and direction for us to intentionally pay attention and remember God in everything we do. The starting point and foundation of any Rule is a desire to be with God and to love him."[6]

So here is my own Rule of Life, which continues to be tweaked and refined, but at least I hold it before me to guide me on the journey:

Lucinda Secrest McDowell's Personal Rule of Life

1. Practice *contemplative spiritual disciplines* through daily guided prayers/prayer books each morning and evening, which incorporate silence, prayers (including prayer journal), Scripture, devotional reading, and hymnody.

2. Observe *Sabbath* one day a week as a time for rest, reflection, and worship. Twice a year take a personal retreat where I accomplish absolutely nothing except rest, reflection, and recreation in the presence of God.

3. *Study God's Word* personally as well as participating/teaching regular group Bible study for mutual support, accountability, and knowledge.

4. Continue to invest time, energy, and resources in *relationships* with family, friends, colleagues, neighbors, and church community. Look for ways to encourage, support, and connect.

5. Fully engage in all my *work 'as unto the Lord,'* and seek to practice the presence of God wherever I serve or labor. Grow in my skills as a writer, speaker, and teacher.

6. Maintain physical *health* through good food choices and regular exercise. Seek to stay balanced physically, spiritually, emotionally, and mentally.

7. Expand my *global worldview* and discover ways to reach out in compassion, relief, and prayerful redemption to marginalized people locally, nationally, and internationally.

Restoration

I have written extensively on the practices of learning how to find rest for your soul in my book *Dwelling Places: Words to Live in Every Season.* Those short but deep studies of such things as quietness, sanctuary, soul, rest, abide, trust, still, refuge, presence, grow, and more will further elaborate ways to enrich your own experiences of soul care.

Too many women spend more time and energy taking care of others than themselves. Often it's because we feel guilty. To that I would echo, "Put on your oxygen mask first!" Unless we are breathing deeply, we cannot help those who depend on us.

Natasha Sistrunk Robinson confirms, "God has designed humans for sacred rhythms that include rest. Whether it's a spiritual retreat, a spiritually engaging and nurturing conference, a fellowship dinner, or a girl's night on the town, taking time to rest, relax and focus on the Lord is important for our soul's care. We must make life-giving choices to rest and retreat so we can faithfully continue our work and live our lives on purpose for God."[7]

I've often encouraged others to come apart before you fall apart. Recently I opened my new calendar and realized it was *my turn* to do just that. I chose for a month to live quietly, offline, and mostly out of touch. I continued much of my work and daily life responsibilities but did relocate for a time. There is no one formula for such a time of desperate respite. Because mine came at the beginning of a new year, I used it as a time to pray, plan, and purpose for the days ahead. Whatever form your time apart takes, God can use those moments to restore your soul.

Seven Benefits from Time Apart

1. *Rest is good for both body and brain.*

   Most of us know we must rest our minds and bodies but often resist tending to our own needs. Women especially often experience a false guilt about self-care. Late last year I began to manifest being overstressed and exhausted. As I listened to my husband's neurologist speak of how important it is to rest both body and brain after surgery, the thought occurred to me, *perhaps I need to recover from* his *brain surgery.* "When our brain enters the rest circuit, we don't actually rest; we move into a highly intelligent, self-reflective, directed state. And the more often we go there, the more we get in touch with the deep, spiritual part of who we are."[8] After his recovery, it was time for me to do the same. Time apart gave me the freedom to sleep, nap, rest my mind, and actually become more creative and energetic at the same time.

2. *Without the daily bombardment of social media updates, I am free from FOMO (fear of missing out) and the temptation to compare myself to others and comment on everything in the world.*

   I prayed through "A Liturgy for Arriving at the Ocean": "May the stresses of obligation, reputation, and deadline here dissolve. May we find rest in the renewed certainty that we need not be feared or respected or popular or successful or somehow perfect, to be loved by You. There is no striving here at the end of our limits."[9] I recognize there is a place for digital life. But in the absence of it, I discovered a healthy balance emerges in recognizing the bright lights of social media often blind us to our identity as the beloved.

3. *Only in silence and wilderness places can I truly hear God's whisper.*

I long to hear from God, but sometimes the noise in my normal life drowns out important truth. It's no wonder He often speaks loudest when we are far from all those things that prop us up. I've learned there is great benefit to just being still—sitting on a bench and doing nothing. God spoke to Moses in the wilderness, and I clearly heard His voice in some wild places during that month. "Wherever we are and whatever we are doing, God invites us to the far side of the wilderness to commune with him. Saying yes to that invitation requires a willingness to step away from the noise, distractions, and demands of our daily life, at least for a little while."[10]

4. *Vital connections are made during face-to-face time with loved ones and significant friends.*

Perhaps the best parts of my month were actually spent in community. Drs. Henry Cloud and John Townsend encourage deep relationships with those who 1) draw us closer to God, 2) draw us closer to others, and 3) draw us closer to our authentic selves.[11] If you are married, time with your spouse is always a priority and a privilege. After surviving a challenging year, Mike and I were grateful for time together to reflect, renew, and recharge. I also spent a week (for the eleventh year in a row) in prayer and fellowship with godly women friends who know me well.

5. *I find wisdom in embracing the paradox of productivity during such a season.*

During this time apart I chose to set aside my work, even though I was on a book deadline. I had to realize that though few words were written, many words were being lived out and others marinating for eventual release. It only seemed like I was doing nothing—deep down God was still working. "To remain healthy, our souls need solitude with no agenda, no distractions, no noise. If someone asks you what you did in your 'time apart,' the correct response should be 'Nothing.' Doing nothing does wonders for the soul."[12] As with much of life, there is often more going on than is outwardly evident. My rest was productive . . . eventually.

6. *My prayer life becomes richer when I have the freedom of fewer to-do lists competing for my attention.*

For someone who occasionally struggles with focus while praying, a time apart can provide (mostly) uninterrupted spaces and seasons to pray continually. I also love to pull out treasured prayer books and lift up words prayed through the centuries, which help quiet and deepen my prayerful conversations with God. While at the beach I turned to this prayer:

Leave me alone with God as much as may be.

As the tide draws the waters close in upon the shore,

Make me an island, set apart,

Alone with You, O God, holy to You.

Then with the turning of the tide

Prepare me to carry Your presence to the busy world beyond,

The world that rushes in on me,

Till the waters come again and take me back to You.

—Saint Aidan of Lindisfarne (c. AD 590–651)[13]

7. *Words and songs of gratitude became my mantra.*

Over and over I thanked God not only for all He continues to *give* and *do* and *be* for me but also for the absolute undeserved grace gift of this time apart. Though I've always read at least one Psalm a day, I've been inspired to dig even deeper in this amazingly poetical and praiseworthy book. A dying woman once told my author friend Barbara Mahany, "If you love the life you have, please, please, practice gratitude. Wake up every morning

acknowledging just how much beauty is in your world. Pay attention to it, honor it and keep your heart and your eyes wide open.
You won't regret it."[14] Yes, thank You!

Transformation

We must learn how to dwell deep if we are to be conformed to His image.
As we increasingly become women of deep soul strength, we will change.
Actually we will be transformed. As C. S. Lewis put it in *Mere Christianity*, "For mere improvement is not redemption, though redemption always
improves people even here and now and will, in the end, improve them to
a degree we cannot yet imagine. God became man to turn creatures into
sons: not simply to produce better men of the old kind but to produce a
new kind of man. It is not like teaching a horse to jump better and better
but like turning a horse into a winged creature. Of course, once it has got
its wings, it will soar over fences which could never have been jumped and
thus beat the natural horse at its own game."[15]

As you consider your own journey of going deeper with God, what are some
transformational changes you have already seen in your life and behavior?

_____

_____

_____

_____

_____

Where are you still seeking God to transform you from the inside out?

_____

_____

_____

_____

_____

If you were to become a winged creature and soar, what would that look like?

_____

_____

_____

_____

_____

_____

_____

The best benefit from dwelling deep is that God restores balance to our lives. "Life from the Center is a life of unhurried peace and power. It is simple. It is serene. It is amazing. It is triumphant. It is radiant."[16]

Don't you want your own life to be simple, serene, triumphant, and radiant—full of unhurried peace and power?

Soul care will change us. For good. Richard Foster speaks of dwelling deeply in his book *Prayer*. I think this is truly the evidence of a transformed life. "We now begin to think with love. Our decisions become increasingly bathed in a loving rationality. . . . We become, for example, more sensitive to the hurts and sufferings of others. We walk into a room and quickly know who is sad or lonely or dealing with a deep, inexpressible sorrow. In such a case we are able to slip over beside them and sit in silence, bringing comfort and understanding and healing, knowing that 'deep calls to deep' (Psalm 42:7)."[17]

Knowing God

Nothing spurs spiritual growth as much as getting to know God's attributes and character. One way to do this is through a biblical study of the Old Testament names of God and the New Testament names of Jesus. As you look up each passage, note the name of God used in that verse and the name in its original language listed here. Take time to jot down how that particular characteristic and name speaks into your own life right now.

Old Testament Names of God, Celebrating His Attributes and Character

Adonai: Lord (Isaiah 6:1–8)

_____

_____

_____

Elohim: Mighty One (Genesis 1:1–24)

_____

_____

_____

El-Roi: God Who Sees (Genesis 16:13)

_____

_____

_____

El-Shaddai: All-Sufficient One (Genesis 17:1)

_____

_____

_____

_____

Jehovah-Jireh: God Will Provide (Genesis 22:14)

_____

_____

_____

_____

Jehovah-Rapha: God Heals (Exodus 15:26)

_____

_____

_____

Jehovah-Shalom: God Is Our Peace (Judges 6:24)

_____

_____

_____

Yahweh: I Am (Exodus 3:1–14)

_____

_____

_____

New Testament Names of Jesus, Celebrating His Attributes and Character

Alpha and Omega: Revelation 22:13

_____

_____

_____

_____

Bread of Life: John 6:35

_____

_____

_____

_____

Good Shepherd: John 10:11

_____

_____

_____

I Am: John 8:58

_____

_____

_____

Immanuel: Matthew 1:23

_____

_____

_____

King of Kings: 1 Timothy 6:15

_____

_____

_____

Lamb of God: John 1:29

_____

_____

_____

Light of the World: John 8:12

_____

_____

_____

Lord of All: Acts 10:36

_____

_____

_____

Resurrection and Life: John 11:25

_____

_____

_____

Savior: Luke 2:11

_____

_____

_____

Way, Truth, and Life: John 14:6

_____

_____

_____

Word of Life: 1 John 1:1

_____

_____

_____

Serenity and Strength

My word for the past year year was _serenity._ I asked God to help me learn to both rest in and rise above all the outside entanglements that daily threaten my interior life and spill over into my exterior life. The pursuit of both serenity and strength has become a particular passion of mine in this season of life. These guidelines help keep me focused amidst the clamor of all that would bring stress, not serenity.

> But blessed is . . . the woman who sticks with GOD. . . . serene and calm through droughts, bearing fresh fruit every season.
>
> —Jeremiah 17:7–8 *The Message*

A Person of Serenity is:

Still

One who realizes that many problems can be solved simply by slowing down and seeking silence. Hurry is the great enemy of soul care, so she deliberately takes precious time to be still.

Established

One who knows who she is. Her primary identity is not based on her roles in life or specific hats she wears but on the fact that she is God's beloved and is therefore known, seen, and called. This gives her beautiful confidence.

Restored

One who has walked through challenge and suffering, emerging on the other side renewed and refreshed. She has worked through the healing process, allowing God to repurpose her pain and restore her worth.

Empowered

One who knows ultimate power is from God through the Holy Spirit. While deliberately seeking a healthy physical life, she also knows inner strength comes through daily disciplines and spiritual practices.

Nurtured

One who places a priority on that which nurtures her creativity and her soul, like nature walks, a cup of hot tea on fine china, reading that challenges both her mind and spirit, cozy moments with friends, music, and laughter.

Inspired

One who continually consults God's Word for wisdom and guidance. She finds inspiration through stories of both saints and sinners, discovering courage to radically serve a hurting world in Jesus' name.

Thankful

One who knows the source of all gifts and turns to God in daily gratitude. She makes note of His many blessings because, "Who can ever praise him enough?" (Psalm 106:2).

Yielding

One who is willing to surrender all her plans and purposes into the hands of a sovereign God. She learns to hold everything loosely as God gives and takes away. She is resilient and steadfast amidst many changes.

The consecrated life is set apart for God's use. At the conclusion of a retreat or conference, I often lead the women in this prayer of consecration:

Lord, I'm Yours. Whatever the cost may be, may Your will be done in my life. I realize I'm not here on earth to do my own thing or to seek my own fulfillment or my own glory. I'm not here to indulge my desires, to increase my possessions, to impress people, to be popular, to prove I'm somebody important, or to promote myself. I'm not here even to be relevant or successful by human standards. I'm here to please You.

I offer myself to You, for You are worthy. All that I am or hope to be, I owe to You. I'm Yours by creation, and every day I receive from You life and breath and all things. And I'm Yours because You bought me, and the price you paid was the precious blood of Christ. You alone, the Triune God, are worthy to be my Lord and Master. I yield to You, my gracious and glorious heavenly Father; to the Lord Jesus who loved me and gave Himself for me; to the Holy Spirit and His gracious influence and empowering.

All that I am and all that I have I give to You.

I give You my rebellion in me, which resists doing Your will. I give You my pride and self-dependence, which tell me I can do Your will in my own power if I try hard enough. I give You my fears, which tell me I'll never be able to do Your will in some areas of my life. I consent to let You energize me . . . to create within me, moment by moment, both the desire and the power to do Your will.

I give You my body and each of its members . . . my entire inner being; my mind, my emotional life, my will . . . my loved ones . . . my marriage or my hopes for marriage . . . my abilities and gifts . . . my strengths and weaknesses . . . my health . . . my status (high or low) . . . my possessions . . . my past, my present, and my future . . . when and how I'll go home to be with You.

I'm here to love You, to obey You, to glorify You. O my Beloved, may I be a joy to You!

—Ruth Myers, *A Treasury of Praise*[18]

Becoming Soul Strong

Do you have a plan or strategy for dwelling deep? Just as we carve out time for the priority appointments and responsibilities in our lives—perhaps even recording them in a planner or calendar—so we must do for our spiritual life.

Consider how you begin your day. When would be a good time to set aside for prayer and Bible reading?

_____

_____

_____

_____

_____

What location works best for you?

_____

What materials would you want with you at that time? (I carry in a basket my Bible, prayer journal, hymnal, devotional readings, pen, and handkerchief.)

_____

_____

_____

Which elements would you like to include in your own morning ritual? (Elements could include playing soft music, silence, singing a hymn, lighting a candle, kneeling in prayer, writing prayers in a journal, etc.)

_____

_____

_____

Now, as Saint Benedict says, "Always begin again." When will you begin this spiritual discipline?

_____

Write a prayer of commitment where you offer your intentions to draw deep with God each day on a regular basis.

_____

_____

_____

_____

_____

_____

Chapter 4

Pray Always

I live a praying life, bringing all to the God who answers.

As I was driving through Seattle traffic, a loud siren blew, prompting me to immediately utter a short prayer for the first responders and those in crisis.

From the back seat came a panicked little voice, "Don't close your eyes, Mama!"

I had just married, moved to Seattle, and adopted three littles who were suddenly horrified at their new mama praying while driving in traffic. I assured my kids I didn't close my eyes when I was praying while driving. Or walking. Or on the phone.

But I did warn them to be alert because I pray pretty much anywhere anytime.

I learned this practice from my seminary advisor Dr. J. Christy Wilson. Whenever someone gave him a prayer request, he would stop everything and say, "Let's just pray about that right now." I remember feeling awkward at first when he paused in the middle of the cafeteria to pray with me for my mother's surgery. But I learned.

Dr. Wilson's spontaneous prayer was contagious among the seminarians . . . and often the source of a bit of fun. Once while in the middle of a large lecture hall a student started dozing off, and the guy sitting next to him nudged and said, "Dr. Wilson just asked you to pray." Which was completely plausible, though not actually true at the time.

Awakening quickly, the guy stood up in the middle of class and gave a heartfelt prayer. Totally unfazed, Dr. Wilson thanked him and continued the lecture.

I learned from Dr. Wilson that prayer is not just something you do occasionally. Prayer is a way of life. And I discovered that as I prayed about anything and everything, I began to *live* that praying life.

My husband and I sent our children off to school each day with a blessing and prayer, as well as a blessing and prayer for their teachers by name. After all they would be with them for the entire day. It became a holy habit. And to this day I try to pray with my kids whenever I conclude a phone conversation or visit.

Because many years later after that first traffic prayer, my son Tim worked his way through college serving the Lookout Mountain, Tennessee, Fire Department. And one day he told me, "Every time we go out on a call with sirens blasting, I wonder if there's a mama and her kids praying for us."

You can't make this stuff up. Children are always watching and listening—more is caught than taught.

When the Apostle Paul admonished us in Scripture to "never stop praying" (1 Thessalonians 5:17), he knew our lives would be full of many other things—people, work, play. He also knew that in the midst of cleaning house, running a business, changing diapers, driving carpool, teaching class, mowing lawns, or riding the subway, we could still maintain a prayerful posture.

Bible teacher Jennifer Kennedy Dean calls this living the praying life. She says, "A praying life is a life always in active and intentional cooperation with God; a life in which an undercurrent of prayer is always present; a life of continual interaction with the spiritual realm. A praying life is open to the power and provision of God."[1]

If prayer is at its core a conversation with God, then certainly we recognize that conversations take place in many ways. In our own praying lives, we are urged to have daily time of focused prayer and study. For me, this is usually early in the morning before my to-do lists, devices, and people clamor for attention. I also seek to focus at the end of the day on a prayer of reflection, reviewing my part and God's part in the past hours and entrusting all I love into His care.

But what about in-between? When I'm not necessarily sitting, reading, or singing, I remember people and circumstances before the throne of grace through prayers. Sometimes I just whisper someone's name, and God knows his or her needs at that moment. Other times I shoot up arrow prayers—two perennial favorites are "Help!" and "Thanks." And yes, I do stop and pray with people on the phone, at a meeting, walking together, at a table, and through a church prayer chain.

Every moment of the day can become a prayer prompt. Richard Foster says, "In the most natural and simple way possible we learn to pray our experiences by taking up the ordinary events of everyday life and giving them to God."[2]

I pray spontaneously when called upon and sometimes when not. But I also pray often using ancient prayers downloaded directly from the Holy Spirit to the quill or scroll of someone who put into words exactly how I desire to communicate with my Heavenly Father at that moment. I'm so grateful to have access to these anointed prayers from godly believers who lived long ago but seem to understand my twenty-first century soul. I pray Scripture and insert personal pronouns.

I delight in the great variety of ways to embrace a praying life, and I certainly don't intend to foist my choices upon you. However I will share some things that have helped me along the journey with the hopes that you too might be encouraged to experience even more of the incredible power of prayer in your life.

Begin Your Day with a Prayer Offering

I begin each day early so I can settle into my cozy spot wrapped in a soft throw (it's cool most mornings here in New England) and clutching a hot cup of strong coffee. My basket holds my journaling Bible, hymnal, prayer book, devotional readings, and prayer journal. Sometimes I light a scented candle. I don't listen to music. Just that peaceful silence before anyone else has awakened. I am more receptive to God's whisper in the early morning hours, it seems.

> Listen to my voice in the morning, LORD. Each morning I bring my requests to you and wait expectantly.
>
> —Psalm 5:3 NLT

As I enter into prayer, I will often sing the words of a hymn, such as this one.

> Be thou my vision, O Lord of my heart;
> Naught be all else to me, save that thou art—
> Thou my best thought by day or by night;
> Waking or sleeping, Thy presence my light.
>
> Be thou my wisdom, and Thou my true word;
> I ever with Thee and Thou with me, Lord;
> Thou my great Father, I Thy true son;
> Thou in me dwelling, and I with Thee one.
>
> —Irish Hymn, circa AD 700

Each morning I pray through prayers, Scripture, and psalms centered on the church calendar, where each element of life is offered to God. This is referred to as praying the Daily Office—an ancient practice of using prayer to mark times of the day and express the traditions of the praying community, especially morning and evening prayers. (For instance, I don't need a special day to pray for our president. I pray for the president and all those in authority daily.) Here's a morning prayer I keep taped in my planner for travel or missed devotions. I feel it captures all the necessary areas to give to God first thing each day, including the Lord's Prayer.

> *Morning Prayer*
>
> Lord, open our lips. And our mouth shall proclaim your praise. We have come together in the presence of Almighty God our heavenly Father, to set forth his praise, to hear His holy Word, and to ask, for ourselves and on behalf of others, those things that are necessary for our life and our salvation.
>
> Most merciful God, we confess that we have sinned against you this day, in thought, word, and deed, by what we have done, and by what we have left undone. We have not loved you with our whole heart; we have not loved our neighbors as ourselves. We are truly sorry and we

humbly repent. For the sake of your Son Jesus Christ, have mercy on us and forgive us, that we may delight in your will, and walk in your ways, to the glory of Your Name.

We Your servants give You humble thanks, Almighty God, for all Your gifts so freely bestowed upon us, and all whom You have made: We bless You for our creation, preservation, and all the blessings of life; above all, for the redemption of the world by our Lord Jesus Christ, for the hope of glory and for the means of grace. We thank You, O Lord.

Grant us such an awareness of Your mercies, we pray, that with truly thankful hearts, we may give You praise, not only with our lips, but in our lives, by giving up ourselves for Your service, and by walking before You in holiness and righteousness all our days. . . .

We offer prayers for all those with whom we share the Journey: those who have been given to us, and to whom we have been given, those to whom we promised our faithfulness and prayers . . . especially
_____. Lord, have mercy . . .

We entrust all who are dear to us to Your never-failing love and care, for this life and for the life to come; knowing that You will do for them far more than we can desire or pray for. *Amen.*

With all Your people on earth, and as our Saviour Christ has taught us, we are bold to say: *Our Father . . .*

Thanks be to God—Creator, Redeemer, and Giver of Life. We go in peace to love and serve the Lord, and to live our lives so that those to whom love is a stranger will find in us generous friends. *Amen.*

—Robert Benson, *Daily Prayer*[3]

I also pray extemporaneously and find that using the acronym TRIP helps me focus on four key elements of prayer:

Thanksgiving
Begin your morning by thanking God, the giver of all good gifts.
Read Scripture, psalms, a devotion, or a Bible reading guide.
Keep a gratitude list.

Repentance

Start each new day with a clean slate. Tell God where you have failed Him, and then ask and receive His forgiveness. Make the choice to move forward in a new direction.

Intercession

Pray over the names of family, friends, neighbors, and leaders. As you intercede for the suffering around the world, wars, recent devastation, political concerns, church, or work challenges, always end, "Thy will be done."

Petition

Finally, offer your own concerns to God and ask for His provision and power. Give Him your schedule for the day, asking that interruptions be transformed into divine appointments.

The most important thing about prayer is to *do it*. But I find that making lists and consulting the Book of Psalms (God's prayer book) as well as ancient prayers help me focus each morning and beyond. I have discovered there is nothing that can refresh, revive, and support me daily as praying both in the morning and night.

My paternal grandfather went to Princeton Seminary during World War I, and I was privileged to receive his personal copy of John Baillie's *Diary of Private Prayer*. Even with the formal language, it is a small volume I often turn to for prayer.

Here am I, O God . . . lifting up heart and voice to Thee. . . . It is Thou who dost keep in Thy grasp the threads of this day's life and who alone knowest what lies before me to do or to suffer. But because Thou art my Father, I am not afraid. . . . What I desire for myself I cannot attain, but what Thou desirest in me Thou canst attain for me. . . . Dear Father, take this day's life into Thine own keeping. Control all my thoughts and feelings. Direct all my energies. Instruct my mind. Sustain my will. Take my hands and make them skillful to serve Thee. Take my feet and make them swift to do Thy bidding. Take my eyes and keep them fixed upon Thine everlasting beauty. Take my mouth and make it eloquent in testimony to Thy love. Make this a day of obedience, a day of spiritual joy and peace. Make this day's work a little part of the work of the Kingdom of my Lord Christ, in whose name these my prayers are said. Amen. —John Baillie, *A Diary of Private Prayer*[4]

End Your Day in Prayerful Reflection

One way to pray at the end of the day is to reflect on God's presence in your life. More than four hundred years ago Saint Ignatius of Loyola encouraged a practice known as the *Examen*. Here is a simple guideline I have adapted for my own nightly prayers.

1. *Become aware of God's presence.*

   Reflect on each event of the day, calling upon the Holy Spirit to open your eyes to understanding all that occurred.

2. *Review the day with gratitude.*

   As you mentally walk through your day, take time to thank God for His presence and all the joys, delight, and gifts you received. Think of each person you encountered and what you both gave and received in their presence. Review moments of serendipity, nature, food, and other lovely details.

3. *Pay attention to your emotions.*

   Reflect on how you felt that day—the triggers to exasperation or anger, hope or happiness. Did you struggle with depression or agonize over how to do something with the compassion and sympathy you felt in a situation? Ask for discernment to know how to channel your emotions wisely. Note your sin—the times you chose your own way and not God's way—and confess it before the Lord, receiving fresh forgiveness. Use uneasiness to consider the direction God may be pointing. Pray for guidance.

4. *Choose one feature of the day and pray from it.*

   Ask the Holy Spirit to direct you if at all possible to one significant occurrence that may seem positive or negative. Use that as a focus of prayer—intercession, praise, repentance, or gratitude.

Sometimes this focus will be a strong nudge to pray for a specific person. God will show the way.

5. *Look toward tomorrow.*

Ask God to give you light for tomorrow's challenges. In your anticipation are you worried, doubtful, excited, or fearful? Turn each feeling into prayer as you entreat God for His continued strength and wisdom to face all that comes your way.

At the end of the day I always ask the question, "Have I loved well?" an idea I came across while reading Ken Gire. I find it brings me back to the essentials. I then close my prayer time by praying over the names of my loved ones.

Praying for Your Family

God knows our deepest desires, but He wants us to share them with Him. When I pray specifically, I always conclude with "Thy will be done" because, even if I have great suggestions for how He could answer my prayers, I know God sees the bigger picture, and I can trust Him. Often I have prayed too small, and His answer was overwhelmingly more than I could have imagined.

Perhaps my most specific prayers were when I prayed (literally for years) to be a wife and mother, "If it be Your will, Lord." Nearing my thirties, I was discouraged and had thus taken a whole weekend prayer retreat on the matter. The result from my time alone was a list of twenty-four characteristics I was praying for in a husband! I still have that wrinkled and torn page today:

- Strong commitment to the Lord; good theology; able to verbalize and share faith
- Has a vision for reaching the unreached
- From a Christian family
- World Christian—open to missions and has traveled abroad
- Strong spiritual leader and would easily take that role in our marriage and family
- Would see my spiritual strengths, gifts, and commitments as positive, not as threat

- Wants children and willing to spend significant time as a father raising them
- Committed to trying to live as simply as we can
- Knows how to budget money and handle financial affairs
- Believes in having an open home and extending hospitality to others
- Honest and open—a good communicator
- Believes in this priority system: #1: God, #2: Family, #3: Ministry/vocation
- Loves me just the way I am but wants to help and encourage me to become the woman God made me to be
- Communicates openly to me—able to be vulnerable
- Strong yet gentle
- Thinks I'm beautiful (I suppose this also means he needs glasses)
- Intelligent (at least college graduate)
- Doesn't care if I'm not super athletic; likes me to be feminine
- Feels comfortable with my family
- Good sense of humor
- Committed to tithing at least 10 percent to the Lord's work
- Knows manners and common courtesies
- Likes to spend time outdoors
- Has never been married before

I cannot begin to tell you how many times I prayed through this list, usually in tears. I will tell you that during those years I refused to put my life on hold. I went around the world twice, speaking and ministering. I attended dozens of weddings and sought to grow as a godly woman. My sisters had children, and I loved being a favorite aunt.

I know now that God was using this time to prepare me to be *soul strong* for what His answer to my prayers would be. And, if you are in the waiting room for something you desperately desire, be assured that God is orchestrating your life for His own good purposes.

So it was that one day at my office in the San Francisco area I had an appointment with a man from Seattle. It lasted all morning, and when we parted, he asked for my itinerary (because I was leaving the next day for a month speaking in Africa). Several weeks later, when I landed in Tunisia, there was a letter waiting with his request for a date. One thing led to another, and within a year we were married!

The person who was the answer to my waiting prayers *did* embody twenty-three of the twenty-four qualities—all except that last one. Mike was a widower with three small children. I should have known God had something even better in mind—*four* new people to love instead of just one!

Perhaps your own specific prayers have not been answered as surprisingly as mine. I know from experience how devastatingly hard that can be. I've received many answers of no or wait before God finally said yes. And often even the yes answer didn't look exactly as I'd envisioned. What do we do? We keep trusting the one who is sovereign and loves us. We love Him more and more each day. We keep moving forward in answer to His calling. And He makes us *soul strong.* "Yet I still belong to you; you hold my right hand. You guide me with your counsel, leading me to a glorious destiny. Whom have I in heaven but you? I desire you more than anything on earth. My health may fail, and my spirit may grow weak, but God remains the strength of my heart; he is mine forever" (Psalm 73:23–26).

If you have a spouse, write their name here: _____
and make a commitment to pray regularly for him to know God deeply, draw strength and health for each new day, find purpose and meaning in his vocation, love you and your family, be a leader for your children, and serve others in the love of Christ. Hopefully this is a more-than-once, daily prayer by every wife.

In addition to thanking God and praying for my husband, the moment I became a mama I prayed a dedication over my children—that they would know God and He would always guide and protect them throughout life. I gave each child (and later my two new sons who married my daughters and my four grandchildren) the promise that every day when they awakened, I would have already prayed for them by name. Who else will give that kind of gift of commitment and faith? Of course this also means that I must entrust them daily to the Lord—hold loosely even when I desperately want to squeeze tightly.

Who will you gift with a first-thing-in-the-morning-every-day prayer by name?

_____

_____

_____

_____

_____

Prayer for Children

Father, hear us, we are praying.

Hear the words our hearts are saying;

We are praying for our children.

Keep them from the powers of evil,

From the secret hidden peril;

Father, hear us for our children.

From the whirlpool that would suck them,

From the treacherous quicksand, pluck them;

Father, hear us for our children.

From the worldling's hollow gladness,

From the sting of faithless sadness,

Father, Father, keep our children.

Through life's troubled waters steer them;

Through life's bitter battle cheer them;

Father, Father, be Thou near them.

Read the language of our longing,

Read the wordless pleadings thronging,

Holy Father, for our children.

And wherever they may bide,

Lead them Home at eventide.

—Amy Carmichael, "For Our Children"[5]

Prayer for Adult Child

Lord, You have said that if we lack wisdom, we are to ask for it and You will give it to us (James 1:5). I come to You asking that You would pour out Your Spirit of wisdom upon my adult children. Give them wisdom to always speak the right word to others, to seek godly and wise counsel, to be humble and not prideful, and not be drawn toward the wisdom of the world. Help him (her) to have the kind of sound wisdom that brings discretion, so that it will become life to his (her) soul (Proverbs 3:21–22). Give him (her) wisdom that will help him (her) always make good decisions, and to trust the right people. —Stormie Omartian, *The Power of Praying for Your Adult Children*[6]

Do you ever awaken in the middle of the night and have trouble going back to sleep? My husband Mike always prays the Jesus Prayer: "Lord Jesus Christ, Son of God, have mercy on me, a sinner." Recently I have committed to simply praying a name before God when I awaken in the middle of the night. I say, "Mama." My ninety-two-year-old mother lives in constant pain and hardly sleeps at all. And though I pray for her at other times during the day, this middle-of-the-night prayer connects me to her in a special way. This too can be a gift you offer someone special. Your middle-of-the-night prayers. Especially for that person who is elderly, wandering alone, or imprisoned.

Whose name might you whisper in prayer in the middle of the night?

_____

Learning to pray is always a process that will transform us into women of both serenity and strength. But the full embrace of such a praying life is a process that takes time. Richard Foster reminds us, "God does not expect you to dive immediately into the ocean of constant communion and swim from one continent to the other. We move into this way through a process of practiced living that is both understandable and practical. And while this 'practice of the presence of God' is strenuous, everything else ceases to be so. . . . More and more we find ourselves going through the stresses and strains of daily activity with an ease and serenity that amaze even us . . . especially us."[7]

Jesus Prays

Jesus is our model for praying always. We read throughout the Gospels of various times that Jesus went off to pray—"Before daybreak the next morning, Jesus got up and went out to an isolated place to pray" (Mark 1:35). "But Jesus often withdrew to the wilderness for prayer" (Luke 5:16). It seems even our Lord knew the reality of distractions that can prevent us from focusing on God.

Jesus set an example of daily prayer by praying during all kinds of circumstances. Read each passage and record His praying life in each situation:

Matthew 6:9–13

_____

_____

_____

Matthew 14:23

_____

_____

_____

Matthew 26:39

_____

_____

_____

Matthew 27:46

_____

_____

_____

Mark 1:35

_____

_____

_____

Luke 5:16

_____

_____

_____

Luke 6:12

_____

_____

_____

Luke 11:5–10

_____

_____

_____

Luke 18:1

_____

_____

_____

Luke 22:44

_____

_____

_____

Luke 23:34

_____

_____

_____

Luke 23:46

_____

_____

_____

John 6:11

_____

_____

_____

How can you and I follow Christ's example to live a praying life? Only through His presence and power, available to all in whom He dwells.

Prayer is more than an activity or a set of words packaged between "Dear God" and "Amen." Prayer is living in the continual flow of His power and provision, authored and nourished by the living, present-tense, indwelling Jesus. Once Jesus takes up residence in you, He is 24–7. He has moved in lock, stock, and barrel. All of Him in all of you. He does not move in and out. He indwells you.[8]

Prayers

Prayers overflow from what is inside—sometimes those are spur-of-the-moment prayers and sometimes they are pre-composed. Both can be valid. Some believers look on written prayers with suspicion, saying that repeating a prayer makes it seem less meaningful. One man wrote that when he was at a low point in his own prayer life, someone suggested he try a prepared book of prayers using Scripture. Here's what happened.

I discovered that as I prayed along with the words others had penned, it gave a voice to my own feelings, longings, and struggles. I also realized I was not alone but shared the company of many who had gone before me. By allowing structure to shape my prayers, I prayed about things I had not prayed about before, and I was connecting with God around the great themes of the Bible. The result? This discipline produced greater intimacy in my prayers . . . And I learned that the struggles of Christians through the centuries aren't that different from our struggles today.[9]

But just because our prayer lives are personal doesn't mean they are private. In fact the prayers of believers throughout time and all around the world make us part of something much bigger than just ourselves. Every time I pray the Lord's Prayer or a liturgical response I think of my brothers and sisters around the world who are also praying and worshipping.

If you feel stuck in your own prayer life, perhaps you have been trying to do it alone. I'd like to share some prayers that have guided my own devotions in recent years.

Prayer of General Thanksgiving

Almighty God, Father of all mercies, we your unworthy servants give you humble thanks for all your goodness and loving-kindness to us and to all whom you have made. We bless you for our creation, preservation, and all the blessings of this life; but above all for your immeasurable love in the redemption of the world by our Lord Jesus Christ; for the means of grace, and for the hope of glory. And, we pray, give us such an awareness of your mercies, that with truly thankful hearts we may show forth your praise, not only with our lips, but in our lives, by giving up ourselves to your service, and by walking before you in holiness and righteousness all our days; through Jesus Christ our Lord, to whom, with you and the Holy Spirit, be honor and glory throughout all ages. Amen.

—From *The Book of Common Prayer*

Trinitarian Prayer

Good morning heavenly Father, good morning Lord Jesus, good morning Holy Spirit.

Heavenly Father, I worship you as the creator and sustainer of the universe. Lord Jesus, I worship you, Savior and Lord of the world. Holy Spirit, I worship you, sanctifier of the people of God.

Glory to the Father, and to the Son and to the Holy Spirit.

Heavenly Father, I pray that I may live this day in your presence and please you more and more.

Lord Jesus, I pray that this day I may take up my cross and follow you.

Holy Spirit, I pray that this day you will fill me with yourself and cause your fruit to ripen in my life: love, joy, peace, patience, kindness, goodness, faithfulness, gentleness and self-control.

Holy, blessed and glorious Trinity, three persons in one God, have mercy upon me. *Amen.*

—John Stott[10]

Night Prayer

Watch, O Lord, with those who wake, or watch, or weep tonight, and give Your angels and saints charge over those who sleep.

Tend Your sick ones, O Lord Christ;

Rest Your weary ones.

Bless Your dying ones.

Soothe Your suffering ones.

Pity Your afflicted ones.

Shield Your joyous ones;

And all for Your love's sake.

Amen.

—Saint Augustine[11]

Prayer of Confession

Lord, today I confess and turn from:

My insensitivity to those in need . . .

My prejudgments of people . . .

My fear of embracing Your vision for my life . . .

My resentments toward those who have hurt me . . .

My desire to name the terms under which I will follow You . . .

My impatience towards those that believe and act in different ways than me . . .

My unwillingness to humbly listen . . .

My willful choices to do things my own way . . .

My attempts to hide my foolish and sinful thoughts and actions . . .

My efforts to please myself at the expense of what is good and true . . .

My efforts to please others at the expense of what is good and true . . .

I acknowledge that Your ways are good and true, and that it is best to submit to You.

Instruct me in Your ways. Amen.

—Kurt Bjorklund[12]

Prayer for Strength

O God, you are our refuge.

When we are exhausted by life's efforts;

When we are bewildered by life's problems;

When we are wounded by life's sorrows;

We come for refuge to you.

O God, you are our strength.

When our tasks are beyond our powers;

When our temptations are too strong for us;

When duty calls for more than we have to give it;

We come for strength to you . . .

And now as we pray to you,

Help us to believe in your love,

so that we may be certain

that you will hear our prayer;

Help us to believe in your power,

so that we may be certain

that you are able to do for us

above all that we ask or think;

Help us to believe in your wisdom,

so that we may be certain

that you will answer,

not as our ignorance asks,

but as your perfect wisdom knows best.

All this we ask through Jesus Christ our Lord. Amen.

—William Barclay[13]

Prayer in Times of a Sudden Death

Lord, this dreadful thing has happened, and our minds are baffled, our spirits weighed down with grief. It is beyond our understanding why this life should be taken, or why we should be called upon to suffer so terrible a loss. Yet we know that life is full of mystery and that many others have endured the same anguish. So help us to bear our sorrow and not to question your love; for to whom can we look for comfort, but to you, O Lord? Speak your word of peace to our hearts, ease our pain, and lift our darkness. Be to us a very present help in trouble, for Jesus Christ's sake. Amen.

—Frank Colquhoun[14]

Prayer for Our Nation

We have been the recipients of the choicest bounties of Heaven. We have been preserved these many years in peace and prosperity. We have grown in numbers, wealth and power, as no other nation has ever grown. But we have forgotten God. We have forgotten the gracious hand which preserved us in peace, and multiplied and enriched and strengthened us; and we have vainly imagined, in the deceitfulness of our hearts, that all these blessings were produced by some superior wisdom and virtue of our own. Intoxicated with unbroken success, we have become too self-sufficient to feel the necessity of redeeming and preserving grace, too proud to pray to the God that made us! It behooves us, then, to humble ourselves before the offended Power, to confess our national sins, and to pray for clemency and forgiveness.

—Abraham Lincoln[15]

Travel Benediction

May the peace of the Lord Christ go with you,

wherever He may send you,

May He guide you

> through the wilderness,
>
> protect you
>
> through the storm.
>
> May He bring you home rejoicing
>
> at the wonders He has shown you.
>
> May He bring you home rejoicing
>
> once again into our doors.
>
> —Peter Sutcliffe[16]

Will you keep praying always? According to Dallas Willard, prayer is "talking to God about what we're doing together." Thus a life of dwelling deep will include a lot of conversation about your partnership.

Keep living life with God at your side; then you can't help but talk to Him about it!

Becoming Soul Strong

One helpful exercise is to take a long walk praying the phrase, "LORD, have mercy on me." Author Rachel Britton does this often and feels compelled to kneel, as she boldly enters God's presence.

> Coming into God's throne room, I picture myself wearing what looks like a bridal train spread out behind me. The train is everything to do with my life. However, it is not pure and white. Instead my train looks stained and unwashed. Some stuff in my life is not clean. It is heavy, too. . . . All the details of my life—every action, thought, and word I speak—are displayed, like lacework, for God's attention. I ask God to show compassion toward me. The fact God doesn't throw me out of his presence, I find truly amazing.
>
> The act of asking for and receiving mercy is the same for each of us. Mercy requires us to take the same stance before God. . . . My spiritual kneeling symbolizes my heart-felt conviction that I am not worthy before a holy God.

When we ask for mercy, God responds with the same grace to each of us, even though we are all different and no matter the condition of our lives. Grace means the wrongdoing in my life is enveloped in God's train that billows forth from him and fills the temple in which I am kneeling. I am swathed in his grace that shines like the sun.[17]

Why not spend a season in confessional prayer as Rachel did? As you settle into a posture of repentance, repeat the phrase, "Lord, have mercy on me." Feel free to write down your prayers and His answers.

_____

_____

_____

_____

_____

_____

_____

_____

_____

_____

_____

_____

_____

_____

_____

_____

_____

_____

_____

Chapter 5

Overcome Pain

I allow my scars to open new doors of service.

Unable to move anything in her body below her neck, Joni Eareckson Tada sought the only way possible to end her life: she violently wrenched her head back and forth, hoping to sever her spinal cord. It didn't work.

A quadriplegic at age seventeen from a diving accident, Joni despaired at the thought of permanent paralysis. "I hated being paralyzed. But I also hated the suffocation of self-pity. I finally cried out, 'Oh, God, if I cannot die, then please show me how to live!' My prayer was short, but the God of all hope heard me."[1]

The next day she made a choice to face her new life, even as she heard God's whisper, "If I loved you enough to die for you, can't I be trusted with this?" Her decision was to trust a loving and all-powerful God.

What is your own pain?

_____

_____

_____

_____

_____

And how do you make the choice to trust God *with this?* Joni began searching God's Word even though she didn't know exactly where to look for answers. In order to do this, she had to put her Bible on a music stand and turn pages using a mouth stick between her teeth. For most of us, digging into the Bible is as easy as punching an app on our smartphones.

She read Romans 15:13, "I pray that God, the source of hope, will fill you completely with joy and peace because you trust in him. Then you will overflow with confident hope through the power of the Holy Spirit." She discovered—as we must—that as we trust God, the source of all hope, our lives begin to overflow with hope and power. We become *soul strong* through the Holy Spirit. Strong enough to overcome pain.

Fifty-three long years since that desperate prayer, Joni declares that life-transforming hope helped her to find peace with herself, with God, and with her wheelchair, "Suffering was the wide-open window through which God shone his healing grace and infinite hope into my life. And it was my suffering that gave me a richer, deeper love for Christ."[2]

If the story ended here, it would still be remarkable. But it doesn't. What else have those intervening years included for Joni? She chose to not only overcome her own pain but to use her experiences to be proactive for others suffering disability.

Over the past forty years the ministry of Joni and Friends has grown to serve thousands of people impacted by disability worldwide: the ministry has delivered 150,000 wheelchairs and Bibles through Wheels for the World and provided Christian care to 63,000 special needs family members through Family Retreats. They also deliver inspirational media such as the Joni and Friends radio program, television program, and podcast. The organization also equips individuals and churches with disability ministry training and provides higher education courses through the Christian Institute on Disability.

Everyone experiences difficulties that lead to pain. And all we want is for God to fix it. How will we ever make it through this? "In the mix of the unfixables of life, we ask 'How can I be with God in the midst of this? Where is God and does he even care about what I am going through? How can I allow the beauty of the Christ-life to emerge against the backdrop of this difficulty—rather than allowing it to become a black hole that just sucks me into the darkness? How can I experience the freedom Christ offers me when I feel so overwhelmed and trapped in my pain?"[3]

When such questions become our own, our challenge becomes not to just survive and overcome our own unique painful circumstances but that we would embody redemption in the process. That we might—through the sufferings we have endured—be refined and repurposed as compassionate wounded healers to others in pain.

I've discovered four steps each of us could take in order to achieve soul strength and significance in the midst of suffering and pain:

Name your pain.

Give God your suffering.

Do the next thing.

Share hope.

Name Your Pain

The phone call came in the middle of the night as crisis calls often do. Soon we were on a plane flying cross-country to help a loved one make the choice to cross from the edge-of-death into life. This alcohol-poisoning event made it clear this person could never drink again. His first step on the path to recovery would be to admit his alcohol addiction. Not easy but also very simple. Naming the pain opens up the door to take proactive steps. Young, brave, and stronger than he realized, that man has made this alcohol-free choice every day for the past nineteen years.

All twelve-step addiction recovery programs begin with admitting to being powerless over your addiction. Why not utilize this model with your own suffering? Face facts: That abusive childhood *actually* happened to you. That cancer diagnosis means your body *is* rebelling and sick. Your husband *did* divorce you and marry someone else. Your job *was* terminated due to false accusations and gender prejudice. You *have been* unsuccessful in finding relief for your chronic illness. Racism *does* preclude you from being chosen for certain opportunities. Motherhood (or marriage) has *not* happened in your life, as much as you desired it. These are obviously just a few of the wounds some of us carry every day deep in our hearts where no one sees.

I already asked you earlier, but here's the same question. Because naming your pain is an important first step toward healing and hope. *What is your pain?* Take some prayerful time to listen in silence, and then write down those areas of desolation, affliction, suffering, woundedness, abuse, discouragement, or brokenness.

_____

_____

_____

_____

If you are one of those dear people in pain today, may I suggest the psalms of lament—which are really prayers that can be used to speak honestly to God about what you are going through, then turning to God for specific help you know will come. See how Psalm 69 shows us that truly He knows how we feel in such times of suffering.

Here is what I'm going through, God!

> Save me, O God, for the floodwaters are up to my neck. Deeper and deeper I sink into the mire; I can't find a foothold. I am in deep water, and the floods overwhelm me. I am exhausted from crying for help; my throat is parched. My eyes are swollen with weeping, waiting for my God to help me. . . . But I keep praying to you, LORD, hoping this time you will show me favor. In your unfailing love, O God, answer my prayer with your sure salvation.
>
> —Psalm 69:1–3, 13

Now write your own version: *Save me, O God, for*

_____

_____

_____

_____

Here's what gives me hope, God!

Answer my prayers, O Lord, for your unfailing love is wonderful. Take care of me, for your mercy is so plentiful. Don't hide from your servant; answer me quickly, for I am in deep trouble! Come and redeem me; free me from my enemies. . . . I am suffering and in pain. Rescue me, O God, by your saving power. Then I will praise God's name with singing, and I will honor him with thanksgiving.

—Psalm 69:16–18, 29–30

Your version: *Answer my prayers, O Lord, for*

_____

_____

_____

_____

_____

Praying such a psalm reminds me that God knows my struggle, but He also holds my solution.

Mostly He is there to hear my lament . . . and to respond.

You may also find comfort in singing words such as the ones George Matheson wrote when his fiancé deserted him because he went blind:

O Joy that seekest me through pain,

I cannot close my heart to Thee;

I trace the rainbow through the rain,

And feel the promise is not vain

That morn shall tearless be.

—George Matheson, "O Love That Will Not Let Me Go"

Before Paul could write to the people of Corinth about how the God of compassion comforts us in our troubles so that we might comfort others with what we received from God, he first had to name his own struggles, found in 2 Corinthians 11:23–28 (*The Message*):

> I've worked much harder, been jailed more often, beaten up more times than I can count, and at death's door time after time. I've been flogged five times with the Jews' thirty-nine lashes, beaten by Roman rods three times, pummeled with rocks once. I've been shipwrecked three times, and immersed in the open sea for a night and a day. In hard traveling year in and year out, I've had to ford rivers, fend off robbers, struggle with friends, struggle with foes. I've been at risk in the city, at risk in the country, endangered by desert sun and sea storm, and betrayed by those I thought were my brothers. I've known drudgery and hard labor, many a long and lonely night without sleep, many a missed meal, blasted by the cold, naked to the weather. And that's not the half of it, when you throw in the daily pressures and anxieties of all the churches.

He has gone through a lot (the thorn in the flesh isn't even mentioned in this passage) and is thus able to conclude in verse 29, "When someone gets to the end of his rope, I feel the desperation in my bones." Paul's ability to identify with the struggles of others is what helped shape him into a wounded healer.

Look up these passages and write down the suffering that is named:

Joseph (Genesis 39:6–20) _____

David (2 Samuel 12:14–18) _____

Tamar (2 Samuel 13:10–15) _____

Widow of Zarephath (1 Kings 17:12) _____

Job (Job 2:7–9) _____

Jesus (Isaiah 53:3) _____

Woman with hemorrhage (Luke 8:43) _____

Prodigal Son (Luke 15:13–16) _____

Peter (Luke 22:56–62) _____

Martha (John 11:17–21) _____

Paul (2 Corinthians 12:7–9) _____

Faithful who persevered (Hebrews 11:35–39) _____

_____

_____

_____

This is only a fraction of biblical friends who suffered rejection, false accusations, debilitating pain, torture, grief, financial ruin, widowhood, destructive living, consequences of lies, chronic illness, incest, violent attacks, death of a child, and more. But many of these stories begin with suffering and end with significance, just as Paul's did. And just as yours may well do.

> Dear Man of Sorrows, so acquainted with grief, help me not to recoil from your wounds, not to fear touching them or to be touched by them. Help me to understand that in my suffering I am not only nearest to you, but nearest to becoming like you. . . . Thank you for being in the midst of these sorrows, transforming them into blessings and filling them with meaning. Amen.
>
> —Ken Gire[4]

Give God Your Suffering

In 1820 a little girl came into the world already struggling with some congenital sight issues. But while still a baby a doctor improperly treated her eyes, resulting in complete blindness. However, even at age eight, little Francis had made a choice that this pain would not be her undoing:

> Oh, what a happy soul I am,
> Although I cannot see!
> I am resolved that in this world
> Contented I will be.
> How many blessings I enjoy
> That other people don't.
> To weep and sigh because I'm blind,
> I cannot, and I won't!

Fanny Crosby continued writing poetry, eventually authoring more than eight thousand hymns, including "To God be the Glory," "All the Way My Savior Leads Me," "I Am Thine, O Lord (Draw Me Nearer)," and "Blessed Assurance." Historians say of Franny Crosby's influence on both the town in which she lived and died and worldwide that she "was one of the corner stones of Bridgeport and a beacon for other women in Bridgeport, Connecticut. Her creative ingenuity inspired people all over the world."[5]

This woman was able to live *soul strong* because she had offered her life—and her afflictions—to God. Fully released to live, Fanny focused not on what she had lost but on all she had gained. This is evident in her published lyrics, many of which mention light and seeing:

> Great things he has taught us, great things he has done, and great our rejoicing through Jesus the Son; but purer and higher and great will be our wonder, our rapture *when Jesus we see*.
>
> —"To God Be the Glory" (emphasis added)
>
> Trusting only in Thy merit, *would I seek Thy face*, heal my wounded, broken spirit, save me by Thy grace.
>
> —"Pass Me Not, O Gentle Savior" (emphasis added)

> Redeemed, and so happy in Jesus, no language my rapture can tell; I know that *the light of His presence*, with me doth continually dwell.
>
> —"Redeemed, How I Love to Proclaim It" (emphasis added)

Fanny answers our questions even today of what to do in the midst of unexpected (and usually undeserved) suffering. Do we decide to live as victims, paralyzed in pain and sidelined by lies from the enemy? No, instead we offer ourselves as a "living and holy sacrifice—the kind he will find acceptable" (Romans 12:1).

> Fanny Crosby, at the tender age of nine, had begun to glimpse the fact that there was more joy in giving than there would ever be in receiving. And she was broken bread and poured out wine for the life of the world. Only God knows the ripple effect of Fanny Crosby's obedience in the offering up of herself. . . . If we receive the things that God wants to give us, if we thank Him for them and if we make those things an offering back to God, then this is what's going to happen—transfiguration, the great principle of exchange that is the central principle of the Christian faith—the cross. We know that the cross does not exempt us from suffering. In fact, the cross is a symbol of suffering.[6]

What does it mean to see ourselves as broken bread and poured out wine for the life of the world?

I was eighteen years old and a college freshman when I was first challenged to come up with a life verse. I remember spending an entire weekend praying and searching Scripture for words that would continue to be a meaningful calling throughout all the seasons of a lifetime. And I wrote in my new green-padded leatherette Living Bible:

My Life Verse: Isaiah 58:10–11 (NIV): If you spend yourselves in behalf of the hungry and satisfy the needs of the oppressed, then your light will rise in the darkness, and your night will become like the noonday. The LORD will guide you always; he will satisfy your needs in a sun-scorched land and will strengthen your frame. You will be like a well-watered garden, like a spring whose waters never fail.

I think back over the almost half century since I first embraced those words, and indeed God has helped me live those verses, even with all my faltering and failing. I see so clearly now the crux of this Scripture is the great exchange. First to spend myself by offering all that I am, all that I have, and all my experiences that others might be fed and satisfied. Obviously this can only be done through the power of the Holy Spirit. The result becomes that my own night will become like noonday. Friend, I've experienced dark times and seemingly endless nights, but the light has always risen upon me. God has indeed satisfied my needs in a sun-scorched land. He continues to strengthen my frame—though now I'm more *soul strong* than body strong. And what is perhaps the greatest fulfillment of this life verse? When I get to the end of myself and feel as though my strength is drying up completely and I have nothing left to give . . . I am miraculously filled like a well-watered garden.

As Elisabeth Elliot observed about such paradoxes of the Cross, "Life comes out of death. I bring God my sorrows and He gives me His joy. I bring Him my losses and He gives me His gains. I bring Him my sins, He gives me His righteousness. I bring Him my deaths and He gives me His life."[7]

Are there deaths ("minor crucifixions," as author Karen Mains calls them) you need to bring to God today? Death of a dream, a hope, or even a relationship?

Spend some time in silence, just listening for that still, small voice. Perhaps you hear God singing over you with delight, perhaps you hear His whisper of love, or perhaps your pain prevents you from hearing anything at all. Will you write a prayer, offering up your circumstances and suffering into His loving and capable hands? Give your suffering to God.

Dear Heavenly Father,

_____

_____

_____

_____

_____

_____

_____

_____

_____

_____

In Jesus' name, amen.

Do the Next Thing

Amy was living a comfortable life in her home country of Ireland when God called her to the mission field—first to Japan and later to India. While in India she heard a most shocking report of vulnerable children taken into temple prostitution. Little girls as young as five were often "dedicated" to the Hindu gods in India. While living in the temples, these girls' lives were filled with sexual abuse from both priests and worshippers. Who would rescue them from both physical and emotional pain and suffering? In 1895 such things were simply not discussed by decent people. Human trafficking had not become a cause célèbre.

But Amy Carmichael decided to "do the next thing" and answer God's call to help rescue those children. She established the Dohnavur Fellowship and lived in India for fifty-six years without ever returning home to Ireland. In the midst of dark spiritual forces and danger, Amma (Tamil for "mother"), as she was known, awakened each morning, choosing her next thing—whether that be a daring rescue, teaching, or daily chores for the community.

Unfortunately Amma had her life turned upside down by a freak accident—falling into a pit on the property one day. She never fully recovered and spent her last twenty years bedridden and in constant pain. How do you do the next thing when your suffering hasn't ended, when the healing or the answers don't come?

For Amma the choice was to continue as a spiritual mother to her community through her writings. First introduced to her books while in my twenties, I'm grateful most writings have now been compiled into one volume, *Mountain Breezes.* Because Amy Carmichael viewed her life as sharing in the sufferings of Christ, I have gladly quoted her in all my own books.

One of my most favorite poems reinforces the idea that we need not wait until all is well before we serve—but we can dwell, sing, and work even *in the midst* of the pain.

Before the winds that blow do cease,
Teach me to dwell within Thy calm;
Before the pain has passed in peace,
Give me, my God, to sing a psalm,
Let me not lose the chance to prove
The fullness of enabling love.
O Love of God, do this for me;
Maintain a constant victory.

—Amy Carmichael, "Constant Victory"[8]

What is your next thing? It may be something quite ordinary, like preparing and serving dinner or dutifully finishing up that project at work. It may be something simple yet hard, like my friend Vicki who suffers debilitating rheumatoid arthritis but refuses to let it hinder her leading a national health ministry. In our video prayer time last week, she said, "I get up in the morning, put on my workout clothes, and teach the class, no matter how horrible I feel."

My friend Tammy Sue carried the scars of childhood abuse into adulthood but was determined to break free. In her book, *Wounded Song*, she moves into healing through Christ's sacrificial love. "During my search for blame . . . I discovered . . . that when I'm at a crossroad in my life, my journey becomes smoother if I choose to look towards the cross. And without someone to blame . . . who pays for my misfortune? I realized there was nowhere to send the bill because it had already been paid in full."[9]

Now Tammy Sue shares with wounded women everywhere that God is enough for healing and hope and often quotes this verse that strengthened her, "I waited patiently for the LORD; he turned to me and heard my cry. He lifted me out of the slimy pit, out of the mud and mire; he set my feet on a rock and gave me a firm place to stand. He put a new song in my mouth, a hymn of praise to our God" (Psalm 40:1–3 NIV).

What if you don't know what your next thing is?

Sometimes when we are in the midst of our suffering, we are blinded to God's ways and simply must put one foot in front of the other. The following biblical story shows how even being willing to be willing can help us on the path to healing.

Naaman was a respected Syrian general who suffered from a deadly disease—leprosy. Desperate for healing, he sought answers on his own terms and, for a while, got sidetracked in trying to do the next thing.

His wife's maidservant mentioned a prophet in Samaria who could miraculously cure his leprosy. Mistaking her intent, Naaman had his own king prepare an introductory letter for the king of Israel. He did not go directly to the source—the prophet.

How often we think it is the high and mighty—the famous and fortunate—who have all the answers for us? But sometimes God's ways are much smaller and quieter.

Naaman arrived with a full entourage carrying ten changes of clothes, ten talents of silver, and six thousand shekels of gold. But the king misunderstood his letter and lamented, "Why is this man asking me to heal someone with leprosy? I can see that he's just trying to pick a fight with me" (2 Kings 5:7). At this point Namaan was literally left holding his bag of money, which was of no use in his pursuit of wholeness.

Eventually he made his way to the true healer, Elisha the prophet. Undaunted, Naaman showed up in force with horses and chariots, commanding an audience. Instead a servant ran out with the message from Elisha, "Go and wash yourself seven times in the Jordan River. Then your skin will be restored, and you will be healed" (v. 10).

Sometimes the next thing comes in simple instructions. But this one made Naaman furious. He was expecting something profound, at the very least the prophet himself coming out and standing in authority to call on the name of the Lord for healing. Naaman wanted a big splash, but God had other plans for him—splashing in the river. Yet even the Jordan River infuriated this man who looked with disdain and said, "Aren't the rivers of Damascus, the Abana and the Pharpar, better than any of the rivers of Israel? Why shouldn't I wash in them and be healed?" (v. 12).

Naaman was furious that healing had not come in the way he expected and humiliated that others were not doing his bidding. Washing in a dirty river seemed beneath a man of his stature, so he simply refused.

Why is it so hard for us to follow God's instructions?

Naaman's intuitive servants courageously challenged him by saying, "If the prophet had told you to do something very difficult, wouldn't you have done it? So you should certainly obey him when he says simply, 'Go and wash and be cured!'" (v. 13). In other words, if you are willing to do something dramatic, why not be willing to do something ordinary?

Eventually Naaman obeyed God. "So Naaman went down to the Jordan River and dipped himself seven times, as the man of God had instructed him. And his skin became as healthy as the skin of a young child, and he was healed!" (v. 14).

Finally: healing. And Naaman's earnest response reflected his new-found wisdom, "Now I know that there is no God in all the world except in Israel" (v. 15). God alone was powerful enough to restore his life and health.

Are you willing to obey whatever God says in order to seek healing or transformation? What steps could you take toward your next thing, as Naaman did? Write down your own response after each action step:

Recognize your need—something is wrong and needs fixing.
My need is

_____

_____

_____

Be open to receiving advice and direction from unexpected sources.
Possible sources of guidance are

_____

_____

_____

Begin a journey in the direction of where the help lies—possibly a spiritual quest toward the God of all healing or a medical or emotional path through professional help.
I will seek help from

_____

_____

_____

Trust God and do what He says, even if it makes no sense to you.
I will trust God's words to

_____

_____

_____

Thank God and proclaim that He is worthy.
Thank You, God, for

Share Hope

"I don't really trust anyone without a limp." I once remarked to a friend.

What I meant was that those who have been broken or wounded live differently from those for whom life is a constant picnic. We don't offer pat answers. We listen for what is going on behind the spoken words. We move forward each day even if our healing process is not yet complete. Our limp serves as a metaphor to show that we are real, imperfect people who have learned hard things by following God through suffering.

Because of this path, the hope we offer others is often genuine and true. Redemptive. Time and time again I have discovered that the comfort I received in my *particular* pain transforms into generalized compassion and knowledge that can be helpful to others in *any* pain.

Because nothing is wasted in God's economy.

> My firsthand experience does not terminate in me. It is transmuted so that I become able to deal gently and helpfully with others in their struggles. . . . In suffering, I learned to need mercy. From suffering, I learned to give mercy. . . . The courage to carry on and the strong love that cares well for others are formed in the crucible of struggle.[10]

Malcolm Muggeridge was a brilliant BBC journalist who came to know Jesus in his sixties. His was a life full of every opportunity imaginable as he interfaced with the most important people of the time. And yet he surprised many in reflecting on life lessons when he said, "Contrary to what might be expected, I look back on experiences that at the same time seemed especially desolating and painful with particular satisfaction. Indeed, I can say with complete truthfulness that everything I have learned in my seventy-five years in this world, everything that has truly enhanced and enlightened my existence, has been through affliction and not through happiness, whether pursued or attained."[11]

The Japanese embrace affliction through an unusual concept called *wabi-sabi*, which is the art of finding beauty in imperfection by revering authenticity above all and seeing imperfection as beautiful. One of the ways this is done is by mending broken pottery, not with clear glue but gold-infused glue so that the cracks are actually highlighted.

God wants to do this in our lives as well. In fact the gospel is like spiritual *wabi-sabi* as God redeems imperfect, broken people and uses us to bless a fractured world. When we own our broken places as a valuable part of who we are, then we are better equipped to reach out in grace and mercy to others with the good news.

How can you similarly allow God to use the real and broken areas of your life for His glory?

We don't have to look very far to find others who need this good news of beauty from ashes. Pain, sorrow, and suffering are all around us. When I hear of a cancer diagnosis or a broken marriage, I desperately want to fix, comfort, or solve. Which is often not my place or time to do. What I can do is sit in sorrow and offer hope.

Here's my simple list of what to do for those who are suffering:

Pray: If I say I will pray for someone in need, then I must do it immediately (yes, even on the phone or while driving), but I also write it in my prayer journal for remembering them before the throne of grace over and over again. I don't pass along their request to anyone else (including the church prayer chain) unless I have received permission and the exact wording to do so.

Lord God, in Your compassion, come close to those who cry out in pain, to all who are sleepless with worry, and to any who are physically or mentally wounded. Convince us that what matters in healing is not a magic formula, or a special form of prayer, but simply the willingness to enlarge our trust in Your presence. May Your presence encourage those who nurse and tend the sick or wait and weep as loved ones cling to life.[12]

Contact: Sometimes the best way to connect is through a hand-written note that can be read over again. I collect vintage hand-kerchiefs and slip one into sympathy cards, especially to new widows. It is often more practical to contact by phone call, text, or email to remind those suffering that I have not forgotten and am standing with them. Most welcomed is practical help, such as meals, childcare, gift cards, housecleaning, etc. However I rarely ask, "What do you need?" I just deliver the gift.

Remind: What do I say to the discouraged, grieving, or suffer-ing? I share my story, not in an attempt to top their story but to reveal God's faithfulness over time. I gently remind them of God's love and God's presence—that the Creator and Sustainer of the universe knows what they are suffering and is alongside them throughout the journey.

When musician and author Michael Card played a Christmas concert in my ancient church a few years ago, he sang, "Come Lift Up Your Sorrows," which is a song of lament. It was especially appropriate for Advent, since many are hurting during the holidays. His humble admission to feeling depression even during Christmas reminded me that if I am not interested in your hurts, I am not interested in you.

> If you and I are to know one another in a deep way, we must not only share our hurts, anger, and disappointments with each other (which we often do), we must also lament them together before the God who hears and is moved by our tears. Only then does our sharing become truly redemptive in character. The degree to which I am willing to enter into the suffering of another person reveals the level of my commit-ment and love for them.[13]

Sometimes all we can do is cry. But do not despise your tears. Jesus also wept.

A wise woman once told me, "Don't waste your pain." I know now exactly what she meant. Live *in* your pain and journey *through* your pain in such a way that you become transformed by the experience. Nothing is wasted if you learn the lessons, if you persevere and stand steadfast for the ultimate reward. Suffering is inevitable, but don't you want your suffering to count for something bigger?

It's your choice. Will you become bitter or better?

Abigail had such a choice to make. We read of her in 1 Samuel 25 where she is introduced as "a sensible and beautiful woman," while her husband Nabal is described as "crude and mean in all his dealings" (v. 3). Do you think she knew something of pain in her life with a husband like that?

David and his men encountered Nabal's shepherds in the fields but did not harmed them. So when David sent a friendly message to Nabal asking for some provisions, he was surprised to receive a very nasty reply.

As David took four hundred soldiers to show Nabal who was boss, a faithful messenger ran straight to his mistress Abigail to see if she could intervene. He made it clear to her that David's men had treated all of Nabal's shepherds with kindness and did not deserve this rejection: "You need to know this and figure out what to do, for there is going to be trouble for our master and his whole family. He's so ill-tempered that no one can even talk to him!" (v. 17).

Abigail immediately swung into action with a plan that reflected her godliness, wisdom, and courage. "She fell at [David's] feet and said, 'I accept all blame in this matter, my lord. Please listen to what I have to say. I know Nabal is a wicked and ill-tempered man; please don't pay any attention to him. He is a fool, just as his name suggests" (vv. 24–25).

She then used a bit of psychology to convince David that killing all Nabal's men would not be in his best interest in the long run. "Even when you are chased by those who seek to kill you, your life is safe in the care of the LORD your God, secure in his treasure pouch! But the lives of your enemies will disappear like stones shot from a sling! When the LORD has done all he promised and has made you leader of Israel, don't let this be a blemish on your record. Then your conscience won't have to bear the staggering burden of needless bloodshed and vengeance. And when the LORD has done these great things for you, please remember me, your servant!" (vv. 29–31).

David listened and thanked her, turning away from conflict. A relieved Abigail returned home to a drunken Nabal who had been partying hard. After she let him sleep it off, she explained her actions, which had saved his skin yet again. "As a result [Nabal] had a stroke, and he lay paralyzed on his bed like a stone. About ten days later, the LORD struck him, and he died" (vv. 37–38).

Abigail had accepted her painful marriage and determined to live with integrity against all odds. When David heard she was a widow, he sent for her in marriage, which made her both happy and hopeful (v. 41). But the main takeaway from this story is not that she was delivered from marital abuse but that "she did not allow the circumstances of her life to determine what she would become. Rather than becoming hard, bitter, cynical or stagnant, she allowed God to chisel away at her character, making her brilliantly beautiful against the dark background of a difficult life."[14]

Don't Waste Your Pain

Yet again we overcome pain by making a choice. Will you give in to circumstances of suffering or choose to follow the Almighty God into hope and healing?

One psychologist makes it clear, "Your healing hangs on the hinge of this life-changing choice. . . . It is the choice to find strength in your struggle. It is the choice to find hope in your hurt. It is the choice to choose the direction of your life and the demeanor of your spirit. In short, it is the determination to make the best of the worst."[15]

Let's return to soul strong woman, Joni Eareckson Tada, who concludes her book, Infinite Hope in the Midst of Struggles, with a reminder of the hope we find of heaven. She muses that when she finally has the use of her own arms with which to wipe away her tears, she won't have to, because God will wipe them away.

Mostly Joni would love to bring her wheelchair to heaven, wheel it up to Jesus and say, "Jesus, see this wheelchair? You were right when you said that in this world we would have trouble. This wheelchair was a lot of trouble. But the weaker I was in it, the harder I leaned on you. And the harder I leaned on you, the stronger I discovered you to be. Thank you for giving me this bruising of a blessing. My wheelchair showed me a side of your grace that I never would have seen otherwise."[16]

Don't waste your pain.

Lord, I am going through some really hard times right now. I pray that I remain faithful to you throughout the days ahead, so that my witness brings glory to you. You know what lies before me and are in charge of the whole world, so I trust you for my future. Your eyes are on me—as are others, I am sure—so guide my walk when I falter, Lord. You are not an absent Creator—you show up and coach us through our suffering. When I cannot sleep, I will seek out your songs in the night to remind me that you have equipped me for this very time. Remind me of your commands and teachings written on the tablet of my heart so that I do not fall away and allow doubt and despair to run my life. May I come out of this time of testing a refined believer, so that others see that faith works in the furnace of life . . . and that you lead us out of despair to springs of water that refresh us. In the meantime, help me bear my sorrows and heal my brokenness, so that I can confidently proclaim that you are by my side. Help me not to question the "whys," because I know that my thoughts are not your thoughts, my ways are not your ways, and your eternal purpose behind these struggles is beyond what I can guess. I will consider it all joy to walk through these days ahead, knowing that the testing of my faith will bring about spiritual fruit in my life. Therefore, I pray, Not my will, but yours, Father. In Jesus' name, amen. — Janet Holm McHenry, adapted from John 11:4; Psalm 23:3; 34:13–21; 35:10–11; Proverbs 3:3; Isaiah 49:10; 55:8; James 1:2–5; Matthew 26:39[17]

Becoming Soul Strong

Cynthia bought the greeting card for herself. It said, "Sorry. The Lifestyle You Ordered Is Currently Out of Stock!"

How often must we face such reality—that our life simply did not turn out as we'd ordered?

My friend, Dr. Cynthia Fantasia, in her achingly beautiful book, *In the Lingering Light*, writes of her years as a caregiver for her husband of forty-eight years who had Alzheimer's disease. "While I don't believe that God tests us, I do believe that He allows certain life experiences so we will grow and our faith will be strengthened. There were many times . . . when I wanted to have a conversation with God and ask just what it was that I was supposed to learn. 'Give me a book, Lord,' I would say, 'and I'll read it and learn all the lessons necessary for a whole and complete life.' But a book was not part of the process. Real learning happens only from real experience."[18]

What has been an unexpected pain or suffering in your own life?

_____

_____

_____

_____

_____

_____

What are some of the lessons God is teaching you through this new reality?

_____

_____

_____

_____

_____

_____

One way to overcome pain is to channel those hard experiences into something positive and redemptive. Cynthia chose to vulnerably share the most painful time in her life, "For me, writing this book is my gift to the Alzheimer's world. I pray that through reading about my experience, others will be encouraged and strengthened."[19]

In what way could you make your own pain redemptive?

_____

_____

_____

_____

_____

_____

_____

_____

_____

_____

_____

Father, I am weary, but I struggle to rest, to sleep. The darkness increases my fears because I can't see the road ahead. I want answers; I want control; I want peace. Yet I am learning that You want me to surrender—surrender to You, my light in the dark night. I lift my hand to You and ask that You grab hold and lead me through this darkness. The night always gives way to dawn, and I will hold tight until the light comes—when and how, I do not know. But I know that You know the unknown, You are sovereign, and You love me. Lead me and guide me, I pray.

—Cynthia Fantasia[20]

Chapter 6

Extend Kindness

I become a person who freely shows grace and mercy to all.

I looked around the room at the twelve brave young people who showed up for a field trip to the local community college. Occasionally in my work as a high school substitute teacher, I am assigned the special education "Transitional Academy" for students who are no longer at high school but have been mandated an education until they are twenty-one. This is special life and vocational training on learning how to integrate into the world. Today we will visit and eat lunch at a nearby college.

I sigh as I remember my eldest son tackling all these issues only a few years ago. When you're labeled as "different" in any way it takes courage to show up and explore new life options—like dreams of higher education.

As the students filed in from their buses, I glanced up at the classroom wall to a large sign with a quote attributed to Henry James:

> Three things in human life are important. The first is to be kind. The second is to be kind. And the third is to be kind.

I can only imagine the myriad times these students have been the brunt of unkindness. Whether they were intentionally mocked or treated as invisible, such things are hurtful. At the very least, acts of unkindness erode the confidence needed to be part of a world whose rules constantly change.

And yet, as we loaded up for the field trip, I sensed an excitement and, yes, *courtesy* to one another. Their kindness has already begun to affect me.

Perhaps we really could, after all, change the world with kindness.

Not long ago the cover of *Parade* magazine boasted a bright image with the headline, "Throw Kindness Around Like Confetti!" After observing that our country seems to be in a bit of a kindness crisis these days, the story went on to reveal some statistics. Evidently half the people in a recent survey say that kindness has deteriorated in the past ten years. "There is less kindness in public life, which trickles down and invites people to be less kind in our personal lives," says psychologist Harriet Lerner. "But kindness is not an 'extra.' It's at the heart of intimacy, connection, self-respect and respect for others."[1]

I believe kindness is also at the heart of a *soul strong* woman. It is the base line for much deeper characteristics we are called to live—grace, mercy, and compassion. And it seems the desire for kindness is everywhere. A popular phrase, "In a world where you can be anything, be kind" has popped up on everything from T-shirts to post cards to journals.

We can choose each day—each moment really—to act kindly, to take the high road and not react with indignation, irritation, or impatience. Sadly, this choice to be kind is more often the exception than the rule these days.

Recently I had business at the Department of Motor Vehicles—an outing most people dread due to the incredibly long lines and bureaucratic red tape. When I arrived at the DMV I was directed to a fairly short line and was relieved to hear my transaction would only take a moment. I noted my clerk was a seated man with crutches behind him. He seemed a bit rattled about the form I needed but consulted his notebook and printed it out as I handed over the payment in cash. However his computer simply was not cooperating, even after we switched to credit card. Everyone around him came to try and help. The long delay obviously embarrassed him, as this was his first week on the job.

As I stood helplessly at the counter, I became increasingly frustrated; however I made a deliberate choice to speak kindly both with my words and my body language. After a long thirty minutes, two women from the upstairs office came down and fixed the computer problem. The incredibly relieved new clerk gave me my form, and I smiled and thanked him, "You're doing great! Remember, we've all had a first week at a new job."

That's when I realized that my behavior had been observed. The other men at that counter kept apologizing and saying how patient I was being. Me, patient? Only I knew how clearly my actions resulted from a deliberate choice rather than by default. And yet, as the clerk thanked me for a being a nice lady, I said in my goodbye, "Life is too short not to be kind."

I could have titled this chapter something other than "Extend Kindness"—like "Extend Grace," "Extend Mercy," or "Extend Compassion." But sometimes such words can be intimidating because we feel inadequate to embody the depths of a gracious, merciful, and compassionate person.

But anyone can choose to be kind. Kindness, defined as the quality of being generous, helpful, and caring about other people, opens doors for others to receive virtues like grace, mercy, and compassion.

This concept was reinforced recently as I listened to Krista Tippett on National Public Radio. She said, "What I like about kindness is that it's doable. Unlike those virtues like compassion or even tolerance that you have to cultivate, you can be a lifetime cultivating those things. You can actually be kind to someone even if you don't feel especially compassionate. It can be an act."[2]

Be assured that such acts are noticed. Not just by all the people standing around in a DMV line but by those who live with you, those who you interact with on a regular basis, and strangers who happen to intersect with your life.

A few years ago, everyone was talking about doing random acts of kindness, which is just a lovely idea deserving far more than a passing fad glance. One hundred years ago a Scottish clergyman, John Watson, who also wrote novels under the pen name Ian MacLauren, urged others to be kind and remember everyone is fighting a hard battle.

Do you believe that we are not only surrounded by the wounded, but often we ourselves *are* the wounded? The arrows of judgment, rejection, loneliness, and hopelessness rain down regularly on the average person. So much so that it can seem we are in a battle to just keep going. And yet we rarely know the burdens others carry. Perhaps a bit of kindness could help lift someone's spirit even if we can't totally offload their burden.

Intentional Acts of Kindness

Ann Voskamp recalls a stranger named Matthew who extended kindness to a young woman one day. Credit card declined and debit card at home, Jamie-Lynn shifted the howling baby on her hip and told the clerk at Trader Joe's that she didn't have $200 cash to pay for her cart full of food.

Assessing the situation, Matthew stepped forward, "Here, let me cover it for you.

"Look, you don't have to pay me back," Matthew said as he pulled out his wallet, "Just give it forward."

Jamie-Lynn agreed and scribbled down his name and workplace so she could thank him eventually.

The next week she called his place of work and told his boss she wanted to thank Matthew for a kindness he had extended.

"Matthew's dead," he said. "Car accident last week—not far from that Trader Joe's."

Stunned, Jamie-Lynn realized that helping her may have just been his final act of kindness this side of heaven. She determined to do what Matthew had asked of her—give it forward. And she asked others to do the same.

> Glorious people, from small town, back road, and every side of this spinning world, giving it forward. Driving cancer patients to the hospital and donating blood and reading to kids down at the library and having a coffee ready for the mail carrier and handing out flowers at the gas station and buying the milk for the woman in the checkout line. People gave forward the act of kindness Matthew began.[3]

This young man was a reminder of the biblical command to "sympathize with each other. Love each other as brothers and sisters. Be tenderhearted, and keep a humble attitude" (1 Peter 3:8).

Will you reach out in kindness and compassion today? Ask God to especially make you sensitive to those who are different from you.

Compassion is necessary for a follower of Jesus, especially when we consider Jesus' actions on behalf of the marginalized, undervalued, sinners, and social outcasts of his day. . . . While our differences may challenge us, they are also a means of the transformative work God wants to do in each of our hearts, both individually and within Christian community. God uses our differences to mold us as we seek to love unconditionally and develop God-honoring relationships with all people who are made in the image of God.[4]

Be kind and compassionate to one another.

—Ephesians 4:32 NIV

What is one act of kindness you can deliberately choose to do this week for the following people?

That person living with you

_____

_____

_____

That child depending on you

_____

_____

_____

That colleague threatened by you

_____

_____

_____

That clerk at the long check-out line

_____

_____

_____

That voice at the other end of the phone who has kept you waiting

_____

_____

_____

That friend who needs you, perhaps too much

_____

_____

_____

That elderly neighbor

_____

_____

_____

That visitor to your church or Bible study

_____

_____

_____

That relative who doesn't understand

_____

_____

_____

That friend who received a devastating diagnosis

_____

_____

_____

That discouraged student

_____

_____

_____

That exhausted young mama

_____

_____

_____

That homeless person with a sign on the street

_____

_____

_____

That person in your mirror

_____

_____

_____

Did you fill in that last one? Yes, don't forget to be kind to yourself as well. I once heard a woman share a sentence of affirmation she repeated every time she needed a kind word—she addressed herself as "sweetheart." I liked that so much that I wrote my own kind words to say to myself when suddenly confronted with a challenge.

> Lucinda's Affirmation in Tough Times
> Sweetheart, this is hard. Breathe deeply. Remember how much God loves you. This did not catch Him by surprise. Open your hands to both release to Him and receive from Him. You are not alone.

I'm an imperfect person who sometimes gets it all wrong. But when I make a deliberate decision to seek kindness, I know God strengthens me. And I in turn can strengthen others. "Your own glorious power makes us strong, and because of your kindness, our strength increases" (Psalm 89:17 CEV).

Radical Kindness

Christian attorney Bob Goff went to Uganda and began exploring ways he could help people in the name of Jesus. While there he began to understand the prevalent fear of witch doctors—everyone was frightened because of their power and their tendency to use child sacrifice in order to exert that power. Yet no one, not even the government, appeared to be trying to do anything about it.

This American attorney tried a witchdoctor for the murder of a child, and it was a death penalty case. Bob Goff thought he was being helpful and brave.

> But then I ran into Matthew 5 about loving your enemies, and I'm like "These guys are actually my enemy because of what they do." So I had to decide for me, do I want to be right or do I want to be Jesus? And there's an opportunity to be bold, [but] you have to be humble.[5]

Goff started traveling the country and meeting witch doctors. Seriously. He has already met more than one thousand. When he asked the witch doctors what they needed, they nearly all came back with the same response—an education. So he started a school in Uganda to teach witch doctors how to read and write. The only curriculum offered in the school is the Bible and Goff's first book *Love Does*. Goff shared, "One of my favorite images is when I get to see them write their ABCs for the first time on a piece of paper, when they used to be out there killing kids."[6]

As a way to express his servanthood to the Ugandan witch doctors, Goff asks to wash the feet of the graduates of his witch doctor school. This man's love for his enemies is evident through his actions and through his continual attempts to lay himself down before them.

Goff's book *Everybody Always* tells this incredible story and concludes with an intervention: "Even when we feel like we can't muster the strength and humility to love our enemies, the truth is we can. . . . It will be messy. Sometimes ugly messy. You'll also be misunderstood— you might not even understand yourself anymore. . . . You'll grow. . . . As you practice loving everybody, always, what will happen along the way is you'll no longer be who you used to be. God will turn you into love."[7]

I want God to turn me into love, don't you?

Jesus taught about this very thing when He told the parable of the sheep and goats found in the gospels. "For I was hungry, and you fed me. I was thirsty, and you gave me a drink. I was a stranger, and you invited me into your home. I was naked, and you gave me clothing. I was sick, and you cared for me. I was in prison, and you visited me" (Matthew 25:35–36).

In other words, "I was a single mom, and you offered me a free night off. I was new to America, and you showed me around town. I was released from jail, and you bought me steel-toed boots for my factory job. I was wracked with anxiety, and you listened without checking your phone. I was in jail, and you put money on my books for shampoo and a sports bra."[8] And then, to an incredulous people who didn't understand, He clarified by saying, "I tell you the truth, when you did it to one of the least of these my brothers and sisters, you were doing it to me!" (v. 40).

We are called to follow Christ, to do what He did, and to do it as unto Him. In his book on Benedictine life, Robert Benson observes, "The picture of Christ that is given us in the Gospels is clear. If we are going to be like him, then we are to stop by the well and offer water to those who are thirsty. We are to wash the feet of those to whom we have been given. We are to cook breakfast on the shoreline for those who have been up all night. We are to stop in the crowd and try to figure out who has brushed up against us. We are to keep our hearts and arms open for the children when they are trying to get our attention. If doing such things in the world requires that we humbly recognize our call to serve others in all humility, then it is a proper trade to make."[9]

One Anothering

God's Word has much to say about how we are to treat others. The phrase "one another" is derived from the Greek word *allelon*, which means one another, each other; mutually, reciprocally. It occurs 101 times in the New Testament, most of which are commands instructing us on how to relate to other people. These one anothers form the basis for true Christian community and thus, our witness to the world.

Some examples of *allelon* appearing in the Bible are below. Look up the specific Scripture reference, and then write in one way you could seek to live out that concept in your own life with other people. I find it most helpful when I actually insert a *name* (i.e., my husband) or *group* (i.e., my neighbors) on each line:

Love one another (John 13:34)

_____

_____

_____

Honor one another above yourselves (Romans 12:10)

_____

_____

_____

Live in harmony with one another (Romans 12:16)

_____

_____

_____

Stop passing judgment on one another (Romans 14:13)

_____

_____

_____

Build up one another (Romans 14:19; 1 Thessalonians 5:11)

_____

_____

_____

Accept one another (Romans 15:7)

_____

_____

_____

Serve one another (Galatians 5:13)

_____

_____

_____

Bear one another's burdens (Galatians 6:2)

_____

_____

_____

Forgive one another (Ephesians 4:2, 32; Colossians 3:13)

_____

_____

_____

Be patient with one another (Ephesians 4:2; Colossians 3:13)

_____

_____

_____

Be kind and compassionate to one another (Ephesians 4:32)

_____

_____

_____

Comfort one another (1 Thessalonians 4:18 AMPC)

_____

_____

_____

Encourage one another (1 Thessalonians 5:11)

_____

_____

_____

Stir up one another to love and good works (Hebrews 10:24)

_____

_____

_____

Pray for one another (James 5:16)

_____

_____

_____

Show hospitality to one another (1 Peter 4:9)

_____

_____

_____

In this list of one anothers, I chose to include "love one another" first because of its importance. I want to be known as a woman who loves, don't you?

Author Charles Martin wrestled with wondering if everything that Jesus said about love was really true when he said, "What if He really meant what He said? What if my singular command is to love you more than I love me? And if I understand Him, He's telling us that if we love Him, we will do just that. Love like He does. It's proof that we do. That bearing His name and calling ourselves His means loving like He does. . . . The love of Jesus is many things, but at the end of the day it is ultimately sacrificial. . . . If there is no sacrifice, then it's not Jesus' love."[10]

Love Your Family

When Mother Teresa won the Nobel Peace prize, a journalist asked her, "What can we do to promote world peace?" She answered, "Go home and love your family."

All kindness must begin at home. Those of us who are married know that sometimes our spouse gets the short end of the deal. He is the one we snap at because someone else has upset us. We get lazy in our efforts to encourage, respect, affirm, and support him. And yet our default to kindness should begin with him first. As well as with our children. While this is not a book on parenting, let me just say that kindness, as in most virtues, is more caught than taught. If you are kind—full of grace, mercy, and compassion—then your children are more likely to emulate those actions, even if they never use those terms.

Grace-filled parenting is the healthiest way to raise kids. It is my observation that most people I meet around the world share similar needs for secure love, significant purpose, and strong hope. I believe this is also true for children entrusted to our care. We must provide an atmosphere that promotes *security*—assuring them they are accepted and loved, no matter what; offers *significance*—helping them understand their unique gifts and urging them to courageously pursue all God has for them; and provides *strength*—cultivating inner fortitude to keep going in difficult times and placing their hope in God.

We must allow our children to learn the hard way and even fail. To learn that actions have consequences and that choices do make a difference. If we focus more on trying to please others rather than pleasing God, our children will get the message they must earn our favor and others' approval. Instead we should encourage them to rest securely in the unconditional love of Christ and find purpose in glorifying Him in all they do.

Raising a new generation that extends kindness may be one of our most important legacies.

Encouragement

And in those times when we don't know what to say or what to do, one way to give kindness is simply to just show up. Offer your presence.

> One of the beautiful dimensions of kindness is presence. Being present with others when no one else notices is the kind of kindness God sees. It is the quiet gift of being there. Perhaps presence is the most profound act of kindness.[11]

Another way is through silence. Sometimes there simply are no words. Sometimes we just sit beside another person in silence. Are you comfortable in silence? I have learned that by practicing silence in my own devotional times with God, I can learn to become comfortable in those previously awkward moments of silence with others.

As encouragement becomes part of living out kindness, we are often surprised to discover what small gestures and timely words can do in someone else's life.

Recently a young woman asked me to read and endorse her new book. I met her the prior year when she had attended the *reNEW* writers' retreat I co-direct. I appreciated Carrye's creativity and courage and was glad to help support her launch. Imagine my surprise as I'm reading a chapter to discover myself on the pages. You see, as the retreat ended, I had asked to take a photo together.

Carrye writes, "In this simple gesture of choosing to take a picture with me, this woman called me to see myself as her peer, as a writer and as someone worth being with. It may sound silly, but the simple act of choosing someone is powerful."[12]

This young woman's words reminded me that I am now a seasoned mentor with a role to play in lifting up others. I am reminded of a time when only in my thirties God helped me understand, even then, my role as an "older woman."

I had stumbled upon the mandate in Titus 2:3–4 about living in a way that honors God, "They should teach others what is good. These older women must train the younger women." It was easy to dismiss this as something for my mother's generation until the Spirit spoke into my heart. *No matter your age, there are always younger women.* And it occurred to me that as the wife of a college dean of students, I had a whole campus full of younger women just outside my door.

I immediately started a weekly Bible study in my home for college women—yes, even though my hands were full as a part-time radio broadcaster and full-time mama of four young children. As for our gatherings, I know they weren't perfect, and I will probably never know this side of heaven the fruit of our time together. But my obedience to this prompting was the impetus to always keep my eyes open for those I could encourage along life's journey.

I am painfully aware of both my stumbling and soaring as I sought to mother my four quite-different children through the many vicissitudes of life. I am utterly grateful that each survived and is now thriving as their own person with myriad interests and responsibilities. But I also realize that my life's influence goes beyond mothering my own children. I can be a spiritual mama to many throughout my lifetime.

While all women do not necessarily become mothers, I believe all women have the potential to serve as spiritual mothers to encourage others to become *soul strong*. Sometimes such relationships of older women with younger women last for years or a lifetime. More frequently such influencing times last for a season, even for a weekend intensive, such as a conference or retreat.

Intergenerational sharing is important to all woman for many reasons. Those of us who have lived more of life and experienced both suffering and God's faithfulness have many stories and lessons to share with someone a few steps behind. Even though our circumstances may differ, there are universal truths to be learned. Younger women can teach us new ideas, technology, thinking, and trends—making us more sensitive to how to help in their many challenging changes. Our hearts and minds open to experiences we might not have otherwise pursued without their influence.

Does the idea of spiritual mothering sound a bit daunting? Perhaps it will help if you think of it as using skills you've already learned whilst parenting, teaching, or managing a staff. Here are six key actions I have identified as important to those in a mentoring relationship:

1. **Listen:** Get to know someone by truly hearing their heart and not just what they are saying. Be present and truly interested in them as an individual. People are hungry for someone to focus on them in real time, face-to-face. This speaks volumes to their worth.

2. **Look:** Ask God to help you truly see this person as one created in His image. Discover their unique gifting, passions, and skills. Recognize and affirm both the strengths and potential pitfalls in being who they are.

3. **Lift:** Everyone needs a cheerleader. Perhaps you are the one to lift them up and praise the small victories. Encourage through affirmation, good advice, prayer support, and being available. Be their safe haven.

4. **Learn:** Just as you have spent a lifetime (no matter how long that is so far) learning about all aspects of the character of God—trustworthy, faithful, unchanging, sovereign, compassionate, strong, and ever-present—you can now help them learn these foundational truths through sharing your stories.

5. **Love:** Isn't this the key—deciding that you will be a vessel of God's unconditional love and acceptance to another person desperately needing assurance that they matter? Love is full of grace to cover our failures. But it is also full of truth to help steer our paths. You can offer both aspects of love to another person with whom you are in authentic relationship.

6. **Launch:** Perhaps the hardest stage is when the time comes to let go and lessen the intensity of your interaction. Just remember that all you have been pouring into this person's life has built to this point. Commit to pray for them and entrust them in God's capable hands. Leave the fruit with Him.

Look in the mirror. You are an older woman to someone. God will show you the way, and I will be cheering you on. Because we women are definitely called to help each other shine.

Who Is My Neighbor?

When Jesus said, "Love your neighbor," the people asked, "Who is my neighbor?" Jesus responded with the parable of the Good Samaritan and concluded by asking who in the parable served as a neighbor. A man replied, "'The one who showed him mercy.' Then Jesus said, 'Yes, now go and do the same'" (Luke 10:37).

> When we try to love God without loving our neighbor, we cut ourselves off from the 'pulmonary artery' of God. . . . Just as our blood must flow from our heart to our lungs, so God's love must flow out to his creation. . . . We see the face of God in our neighbor, and to neglect our neighbor is to neglect God. . . . It is only through the royal law of love that our deeds of mercy and compassion become a blessing. Without it, try as we might to do otherwise, our serving will always be tinged with condescending arrogance.[13]

Reaching out beyond those in our own tribe can be risky. Have you noticed how difficult it seems to have civil conversations among people with whom we disagree? There are so many hot buttons concerning politics, relationships, social causes, religion, and family that it doesn't take much to be misunderstood or, worse, feel verbally attacked. In such situations we must always remember to speak in love. "We need to be trained and transformed by love, so that love is our first language, our initial reflex, and our emotional default setting," says Lori Roeleveld, author of *The Art of Hard Conversations.*[14]

This calling to speak the truth in love includes the truth-telling we do to people we don't know. . . . We must exercise every opportunity to practice love, while weeding out all attitudes or behavior that interferes with it. Harboring hatred, envy, pride, vengeance, greed, fear, or other sinful attitudes diminishes our capacity for love and prevents us from hearing another clearly.[15]

So what do we do when tricky subjects arise between friends, family, or strangers? As I'm prayerful about formulating my own words in the discussion, I have found it helpful to ask and answer these six questions Lori asks in her book, *The Art of Hard Conversations*:

What's my point?

What do I know about the other person?

What emotion may be involved in this conversation?

What biblical guidelines exist for this conversation?

Is this conversation grounded and timed in love?

What's my plan for following up either success or rejection?[16]

Simply taking the time to process these answers makes me more prepared and peaceful inside about tackling those hard subjects. I force myself to think about the other person first and try to project how they might receive my words through their filter. As trite as it seems, sometimes we just have to agree to disagree. "As servants of God we commend ourselves in every way . . . in purity, understanding, patience and kindness" (2 Corinthians 6:4, 6 NIV).

The next time you are called to serve, pray this liturgy:

O Christ Who Made Himself the Servant of All, I would set my heart and my affections upon you—and upon you alone—for I can only serve others rightly when such service is undertaken from first to last as an act of devotion offered to you. In serving you I am freed from my need for the praise of others. . . . So let my love be sincere, and let my service be fearless, O Lord. . . . I cannot know the end of another person's story. Our lives so often only briefly intersect. So let me be content to minister regardless of visible outcomes, trusting that the small mercies I extend will be woven into the larger theme of redemption at work in the lives of others as you woo them to yourself, drawing their hearts by graces offered, and shaping my own heart too in this process of learning to serve well, learning to love well. Amen. —Douglas McKelvey, "A Liturgy Before Serving Others"[17]

Shine a Light

Of course, the goal is for kindness to become a way of life.

As far back as the Old Testament, our path was clearly set out: "O people, the LORD has told you what is good, and this is what he requires of you: to do what is right, to love mercy, and to walk humbly with your God" (Micah 6:8). Our response is to determine what that will look like today in our own lives and through our own influence. Christ followers are God's Plan A for bringing the kingdom of heaven here on earth. And there is no Plan B.

In the sixteenth century, Teresa of Avila put it this way:

Christ has no body now on earth but yours; no hands but yours; no feet but yours. Yours are the eyes through which the compassion of Christ must look out on this world. Yours are the feet with which He is to go about doing good. Yours are the hands with which He is to bless His people.

So let us be His hands today as we shine a light.

I pray You would give me a heart for those . . . who, for whatever reason, are not in the mainstream of life. For those who lie crumpled and cast aside. For those who are forgotten and ignored. For those who are in some way blinded to the fullness of life. Help me not to turn a deaf ear when they call out. Help me to stop, regardless of what the crowd may say. Help me to give them my undivided attention. Help me to give myself to them as You did—to show mercy, to do what I can. . . . Help me to say a kind word so they may be encouraged; help me to give a gentle touch so they may be comforted; help me to lend a listening ear so their stories may be heard. Help me whenever, wherever, and however I can, to bring light to someone who sits in darkness. —Ken Gire[18]

Soul strong women are kind above all, bringing light into a dark world. It wasn't until I was an adult that I realized my name *Lucinda* actually means "bringer of light." Ever since then I have prayed that God would help me shine His light everywhere I go and to everyone I encounter. I have not mastered this completely yet, but I'm on my way.

Perhaps Madeleine L'Engle says it best: "We draw people to Christ not by loudly discrediting what they believe, by telling them how wrong they are and how right we are, but *by showing them a light that is so lovely that they want with all their hearts to know the source of it*" (emphasis added).[19]

Let us now go forth into the world in peace.

Being of good courage.

Holding fast to that which is good.

Rendering to no one evil for evil.

Strengthening the fainthearted.

Supporting the weak.

Helping the afflicted.

Honoring all persons.

Loving and serving the Lord.

And rejoicing in the power of the Holy Spirit.

—Common Commission
of First Church of Christ Congregational,
Wethersfield, CT

Becoming Soul Strong

Recall a situation recently where you found it especially challenging to extend kindness to someone. It might have been while reading a politically-charged social media post, encountering a stranger on the subway, hearing a disturbing conversation among other moms, or even responding to what seems an unreasonable request from a family member.

_____

_____

_____

_____

What do you think was the precipitating action or emotion that made it hard for you to be kind at that time?

_____

_____

_____

_____

How did you actually respond?

_____

_____

_____

_____

And what was the result?

_____

_____

_____

_____

As you reflect now, what might have been some more positive options for handling that encounter?

_____

_____

_____

_____

_____

_____

And how can you prepare yourself to extend kindness when a similar situation arises in the future?

_____

_____

_____

_____

_____

_____

You are not alone. God will give you both words and actions that reflect His grace and mercy if you will only yield to Him and pray for His indwelling when these situations occur. Write a prayer here:

_____

_____

_____

_____

_____

_____

Chapter 7

Share Stories

I reflect on God's faithfulness with gratitude and hope.

Do you remember the summer you were thirty-one years old? I don't.

I mean, I do remember our glorious wedding celebration on Memorial Day weekend and driving up the Pacific coast from my old home near San Francisco to my new home near Seattle with the *Welcome Home* greeting from my new three children ages nine, seven, and four. I do remember the day we returned from our honeymoon. All three kids got out of school for the summer, and Mike went back to work.

Most everything else after that is a bit of a blur.

You see, God had answered my prayers above and beyond how I could have imagined the script of my story. Having patiently (and sometimes not-so-patiently) waited for the love of my life, I met Mike, who had been widowed three years prior and was busy juggling single parenting and campus ministry. I took on marriage and motherhood all in one single walk down a very long aisle and was over-the-moon happy.

But I was also totally overwhelmed. Every single thing in my life had changed . . . except God.

Thus I have suppressed much of my memory of that summer. Psychologists say suppression "is the conscious process of pushing unwanted, anxiety-provoking thoughts, memories, emotions, fantasies and desires out of awareness."[1] When circumstances in life become more than we can handle, we make a choice (sometimes unconsciously) to forget them.

Today, thirty-six years later, I dig deep to recall those faltering beginnings.

In my fog of memory, I see piles and piles of laundry and hours spent in the kitchen trying to make magic—healthy meals on a budget that were tasty to kids and my new husband alike. I remember registering at the University of Washington for a night class on how to advocate for our special needs child who was a challenging puzzle to me. I know there were fun times like discovering all the wonderful parks and lakes near us, but I also enrolled my kids in just about every Vacation Bible School in the area. I didn't care what church; I needed time alone to take a shower! There were more than a few raised eyebrows from church ladies when I had to consult my planner for my own children's birthdays as I completed the VBS forms. Somehow in the midst of all this juggling, I managed to pass the legal requirements and home study, culminating in my court appearance to legally adopt Justin, Timmy, and Fiona.

Still I felt like a complete failure when after only a month we started marriage counseling. I was disappointed my nearby in-laws whom I had hoped would help through this transition had their own set of medical and emotional challenges that year. Those long days between Memorial Day weekend and Labor Day (back to school) were filled with both too much and not enough.

I wanted to be everything to my husband and children who were still reeling from loss. But I hardly even recognized the person inhabiting my body.

Strength and skills I knew so well were no longer required, and everything I needed now was way beyond my comfort zone. My expectations of everyone around me—but especially of myself—were unreasonable. I was filled with striving and survival. My insecurities were exacerbated by my own comparisons to their late wife and mother who had died all too young.

All my dreams had come true, but I was drowning in them.

This snippet is but a portion of my lifelong story of grace, of coming to the end of myself and finally allowing God to step in and assure me of His unfailing love and acceptance. Of finally opening the gift I don't deserve and can never earn—grace—and allowing it to be the foundation of my life and identity. Of drawing on divine strength to do that which I could never do on my own—vibrantly live what seemed too often to be an impossible life.

I had to fail and fall so God could lift me up and I could echo with certainty, "Nothing is impossible with God." I had to let go of trying to be perfect, trying to be *all*. And I had to realize that God would give me exactly what I needed (time, resources, ability, wisdom, strength) to accomplish what matters most.

I had to both let go and grab hold—to relinquish and receive.

This is how I have spent my years. Living out that story. Learning how to become *soul strong.* Only by the grace of God are those same people still present in my life. They love me deeply and I them.

Early Story Influencers

I truly believe stories shape our lives. In turn we share our stories with others. Here are four stories God used to change my young life—to help shape and form my thoughts, beliefs, behavior, and vision.

The year I turned fourteen a new book came out that changed my life forever—Catherine Marshall's *Christy*. This story of young Christy Huddleston, who left Asheville, North Carolina, to minister to the Appalachian mountain people at the Ebenezer Mission in Tennessee, awakened my love of story, adventure, and the tug of God's call on my life. Christy's story was based on the life of Catherine Marshall's mother—Leonora Whitaker Wood, who lived in Montreat, North Carolina, where I spent much of my young life.

Not only was *Christy* an engaging and beautifully written novel, but it also prompted me to action. By the time I was nearing twenty, I too had ventured out into a wild Appalachian area, serving as a missionary among poor Kentucky children. I lived with no electricity or running water, seeking to make a difference in the name of Christ. Many years later, and around the time I needed to hear her message, Catherine Marshall's memoir *Meeting God at Every Turn* was released and spoke of persevering through loss and disappointment and entering into a ready-made family. Her life story gave me courage.

One night when I was a seventeen-year-old freshman at Furman University, I had the privilege of meeting and sitting under the teaching of Corrie ten Boom. I will never forget her standing before our Sunday night Campus Life gathering and telling her story of hiding Jews in her Dutch home during World War II as told in her biography *The Hiding Place*. Mostly I remember the atrocities of her life at the Nazi concentration camp and her clinging to the promise, "There is no pit so deep, that God's love is not deeper still."

As Corrie ten Boom spent the rest of her life as a "tramp for the Lord" all over the world, sharing stories of His faithfulness and the worth of all people, I felt a longing to become a strong older woman who shares stories. Her experiences of finding worth in those with disabilities also greatly helped me follow my passion in that area for those who are often forgotten.

In my early twenties I read a book and saw the movie called *Joni* about teenager Joni Eareckson, who had broken her neck in a diving accident and was left paralyzed. Her story of going from active athlete to wheelchair-bound quadriplegic in a mere moment of time stirred me deeply. It brought out my compassion and empathy, but even more it made me ask what I would do in such a situation. I admired her courage and fortitude. And this was way back when she had just started her journey.

Along the past forty years Joni's story has continued to engage my interest and heartfelt support. She founded an international ministry called Joni and Friends to elevate the worth and work of people with all sorts of disabilities by providing them with wheelchairs, counseling, family camps, and discipling opportunities. Her wisdom has helped me greatly in mothering my own child born with intellectual disabilities, and I have been privileged to speak at Joni and Friends camps and events. Joni is one of my heroes, and her story gives me hope that no tragedy can stop our spirit. No disease or wound can silence our voice or our influence.

The year I turned twenty-four I began a masters degree program in seminary and found myself lodging with recently-widowed Elisabeth Elliot, of whom I had read in books such as *Through Gates of Splendor* and *Shadow of the Almighty*. These were remarkable stories of a young woman who followed Jesus into the jungles of Ecuador, offering up her own desires for love and marriage. Then, after marrying Jim Elliot and losing him to a violent death, she moved forward in ministry and motherhood. She appeared so sure and so strong. I wanted some of that.

Spending life in her home during my student days—typing her manuscripts and driving her to the airport for speaking engagements—was a personal lesson in what it means to embrace God's truth and do the next thing. I am utterly grateful to Elisabeth for affirming God's gifting of writing and for urging that it was my duty to write for Him. Who knew that more than thirty years later I would be encouraging her daughter Valerie Elliot Shepard to publish another book, *Devotedly*, of more stories through the letters of Jim and Elisabeth Elliot?

These four women—Catherine Marshall, Corrie ten Boom, Joni Eareckson Tada, and Elisabeth Elliot—had incredible impact on me during that formative decade between ages fourteen and twenty-four. It was their stories that initially showed me how to be a *soul strong* woman. What if they had never obeyed and shared their struggles and victories—both through their books and their speaking? I'm pretty sure I wouldn't have written this book laying out seven keys for a vibrant life.

Whose stories have touched you? While these stories may be books you've read or talks you've heard, they may be stories that came your way in the ordinary course of life—people you met. Think back to different times in your life and important lessons you carry. Try to target some of your own early influencers. Though each of these life stages may not be applicable to your own life, use the ones that are as a guideline.

When You Were	Story	Lesson Learned
Young Teenager		
University Years		
Early Twenties		
Starting Work		
Early Marriage		
Motherhood		
At a Time of Change		
Recently		

Backstory

In a book or movie, the backstory refers to the history behind the current situation—basically what happened before that sets into motion what is happening now. To share your story, it is important to process and understand your early life.

When did you last hear a story that spoke to your heart and caused you to make a change in your life?

_____

_____

_____

Who told it and when?

_____

_____

_____

What part of it touched you the most?

_____

_____

_____

Why do you think it caused this reaction in you?

_____

_____

_____

A dozen years ago I took a pilgrimage to the home where I grew up in Thomasville, Georgia. Allow me to share some of my reflections from that experience:

This is where it all began, I thought as I walked the brick pathway to the front porch. Climbing the stairs, I turned my back to the front door and gazed at the expanse of yard before me. A lifetime of Easter egg hunts, soft-ball games, birthday scavenger hunts, kickball, chasing fireflies (we called them lightnin' bugs), and family photo shoots flashed through my mind. The landscaping was different—my mama's meticulously planted flower gardens were gone now in favor of a practical lawn with simple upkeep, but the expanse still seemed huge. Yet I was familiar with every inch—the section of the yard where Barbie and Ken took their camper, the corner where my tree house had been my favorite lookout, and the hill where I went sailing out of control while learning to ride a bike. ("How do I stop it, Daddy?" were my final words before the crash.) It was all here, and a rush of memories stirred my emotions.

I turned back to the front door, took a deep breath, and rang the bell to a home I had not entered in more than thirty years. "Pinecrest" was the only home I ever knew as a child. Our family name, Secrest, had been combined with the tall Georgia pines filling the yard to inspire the name. Every rite of passage occurred here—first step, lost tooth, impossible dream, broken heart, and new adventure had its genesis here, at least for my first twenty-five years.

Today, as part of uncovering my own life story, I was ready to make this pilgrimage alone. The current owners greeted me with grace and hospitality that confirmed what I had already suspected and fervently hoped—this was a loving family home. Still.

My gasp came as I stepped over the threshold and faced the staircase. "Why, it's so small!" I exclaimed.

How many times had my sisters and I hovered at the top of the stairs furtively spying on a grown-up party or waiting to be released to the tree on Christmas morning? How vast the living room had seemed back then.

As I began my exploration I had a destination of primary importance—my little bedroom, top of the stairs and front of the house. Standing by the bed under the window, my eyes filled with tears as I whispered to my hosts, "I saw the whole world from this window." It was true. The bed in that corner had been my haven, my sanctuary from the world, where I would curl up and read voraciously of faraway places, hardly daring to dream that I would one day actually experience them. Or perhaps bury myself in a pillow, crying my eyes out because I felt rejected and unpopular, a nonconformist in a sea of sameness.

I spent hours listening to Rod McKuen poetry records and writing my own poems and stories in diaries, wanting somehow to capture meaning in my musings. This was also the corner where I read my Bible and my very first daily devotions from the book *Streams in the Desert*.

There were times I sat on that bed and hated myself because I felt fat and loud and bossy and selfish. And, truth be told, there were plenty of times I was those things. But there were also times when I dared to believe I was smart and beautiful and adventurous and even capable of being used by God to help change the world. And, incredible as it seems, I really was those things too.

As I bid farewell to my hosts and the house, I could almost hear the barks of long-ago pets Frisky, Rusty, Pepper, Cinnamon, Ginger, and Parsley sending me on my way. This had been a happy place, and my memories were mostly good ones. Here I had been nurtured, provided for, taught, prayed for, disciplined, and encouraged to become all that God had for me. Most of all, I had been loved. Mama and Daddy assured me of their love daily. "Thank You, God, for this legacy of love You gave me," I prayed as I drove away.

Visiting my childhood home helped seal some of my emotions and memories so that I could move forward. Because who we become flows out of who we were.

As you think about the backstory of your life, offer both the good and bad elements to God, and ask Him to help you discern their part in your ongoing story.

On a separate piece of paper, draw a diagram of the home you grew up in (if it was several homes, do the one you have the sharpest memories of). Where was your favorite place in that home, and why do you remember it so well?

_____

_____

_____

_____

_____

Describe the family you were born into (parents' ages and vocations, siblings, house/apartment, church and community involvement, socioeconomic status, etc.).

_____

_____

_____

_____

What values were considered most important in your family?

_____

_____

_____

_____

Are you aware of any long-ago family secrets? If so, what were they?

_____

_____

_____

What was your family's greatest strength?

_____

_____

_____

What was your family's greatest weakness?

_____

_____

_____

Complete this sentence: One of my happiest family memories is when

_____

_____

_____

Complete this sentence: An especially difficult time in our family was when

_____

_____

_____

God in My Story

> Someone once said that God created humans because he loves stories. And the Old Testament tells us about God through the narratives about his people. Jesus told stories and is himself the story of God's outrageous love for us. Stories make up more than 70 percent of the Bible, and it is in the stories of our lives that we can spot God's handiwork.
>
> —Dan B. Allender and Lisa K. Fann[2]

Where is God in your story?

As you journey through life perhaps you can see yourself as Allender and Fann suggest, "We are detectives searching for the fingerprints of God in our lives. We look for traces of his authorship in the rubble of a fallen world. . . . We choose to believe—or at least hope—that our lives consist of more than simply a series of events. Underneath and through each scene lies the hint of a larger story that God is telling through our lives."[3]

When you intentionally take time to reflect on your life—searching for the fingerprints of God—you will discover that it indeed has meaning. Your story matters, and you alone can fulfill the significant role God has for you in the larger story of His kingdom.

What is your favorite Bible story and why?

_____

_____

_____

What is your favorite children's story or book and why?

_____

_____

_____

What is your favorite adult story or book and why?

_____

_____

_____

When was the last time you told someone a story that had a meaning you were trying to get across?

_____

_____

_____

What was the story, and who did you tell?

_____

_____

_____

Where were you, and what was the response?

_____

_____

_____

What part do you hope God will have in your life story?

_____

_____

_____

Is there a step you could take now to ensure that happens?

_____

_____

_____

Try writing your life story in five sentences. I know. I thought this would be so hard, but then I sat down and wrote. Here are my unedited answers:

1. I grew up in a small Georgia town with two sisters and loving parents who encouraged me to become all that God called me to be.

2. As a young adult, I earned several degrees, enjoyed a variety of friends, and traveled around the world twice before I was thirty—through my work in both journalism and Christian ministry.

3. Most of my adult life, even while struggling with a variety of issues, I used the gifts God gave me through communication—writing and speaking—to encourage others.

4. Marrying Mike and becoming a mama of four (three through adoption, one through birth) were both the greatest joys in my life and the calling that most required God's grace, wisdom, and guidance.

5. Because of my many sins of both commission and omission, I live each day under God's mercy and utter faithfulness through His constant presence, bountiful provision, and incomparable power in my life's journey.

Your turn—write your life story in five sentences (you can do it!)

1. _____

_____

2. _____

_____

3. _____

_____

4. _____

_____

5. _____

_____

Say a prayer offering your life and your own story for God's kingdom work.

Messengers

The children's picture book, *I Am God's Storyteller,* helps children understand how God calls everyone to share their own unique message as part of God's kingdom story. It says, "Then came the most wonderful part of that very first story: God created man and woman, sending them to love and care for one another, and for the rest of His creation. God gave them eyes to see, hearts to feel, minds to ponder, and special gifts and talents to share his stories in their own ways with their family."[4]

I love the way this book uses profiles of biblical characters to show that we are all called to be messengers of God's story in our lives. You may be saying right now, "Well, I'm not a speaker or a writer, so how can I be a messenger?" As witnesses to what God has done, our own story may take the different forms of parables, proclamation, and pointing.

> For we speak as messengers approved by God to be entrusted with the Good News. Our purpose is to please God, not people. He alone examines the motives of our hearts.
>
> —1 Thessalonians 2:4

Paul simply carried forth truth first recorded in the Old Testament. Long before Paul, God called Ezekiel to speak, and he experienced some hesitation as well. He learned his audience was going to be a tough crowd—stubborn, rebellious, and hard-hearted. What's more is they had been known to threaten anyone who challenged them.

How much easier it would have been to pass on this one. But he was a man of words—a messenger. As Ezekiel accepted the gig, one final admonishment came from the Lord God Almighty, urging him to not be afraid, "Let all my words sink deep into your own heart first. Listen to them carefully for yourself. Then go to your people in exile and say to them, 'This is what the Sovereign LORD says!' Do this whether they listen to you or not" (Ezekiel 3:10–11).

Basically the prophet Ezekiel was given two assignments: first to allow God's own words to sink deeply into his heart, listening for what God was saying to him. And second to speak to the Israelites in exile (597 BC) with a message of both rebuke and restoration, whether or not they listened.

The measure of his success would not be how well the people responded but how obedient he was to the call. God always provides strength and courage to follow through with His assignments. If the definition of *messenger* is "a person who takes a message from one to another," then each of us must answer this question: *What is the message God has given me to share from Him with others?*

Perhaps you aren't yet sure. You have held your own story close to your heart and are hesitant to unfold it to the world. Because it is a hard message, fragile with pain and perseverance, you sometimes wonder if you have the courage to share it.

Or perhaps you are just bursting to proclaim the good news you have discovered as the Light of the World has infused your own darkness and empowered you in supernatural ways. In your excitement that all may know what you now know, you realize there are pitfalls you must carefully avoid in order to be a winsome witness.

As messengers, our part is to listen to God first then obey the words we are given to share. Why don't we begin by doing what Ezekiel did first, listening to God's voice through God's Word?

Share Your Story through Parables

Prophets like Ezekiel were called to speak hard truths. And in our world today—a culture full of messy morality and vacillating values—we as God's messengers are occasionally called to speak about hard things.

Paul exhorted the people of Ephesus to "lovingly follow the truth at all times—speaking truly, dealing truly, living truly—and so become more and more in every way like Christ" (Ephesians 4:15–16 TLB).

In his book, *Fool's Talk,* Os Guinness says, "We Christians must seek to communicate in a way that is shaped by the One who sends us. . . . God's truth requires God's art to serve God's end. . . . any Christian explanation or defense of truth must have a life, a manner and a tone that are shaped decisively by the central truths of the gospel."[5]

And frankly one of the best ways to communicate in a way that is shaped by the One who sends us is by telling stories. Biblical stories taught through familiar and easily understood situations are often called parables. Our Lord Jesus connected immediately with the people of His time by using parables of their everyday life. Similarly the prophet Nathan chose to use a parable in order to give a hard message.

King David had sinned greatly—coveting Uriah's wife, taking her to his bed, and then arranging for Uriah to be killed in war in order to cover up his sin. With Bathsheba now pregnant, Nathan has been called as God's messenger to confront his king.

Nathan tells the king a story, a parable about a man with a whole flock who took his neighbor's only lamb to feed his guests. Upon hearing this, David exclaimed, "Any man who would do such a thing deserves to die!" (2 Samuel 12:5). Then Nathan inserted the blow, "You are that man!" (v. 7).

Of course, since David had been a shepherd, this parable was a perfect way to break through his blindness and touch his heart. Immediately David confessed, "I have sinned against the LORD" (v. 13).

Why did Nathan use a parable? It would have been dangerous for him to call the king out on his extreme and violent conduct directly, so he led David to recognize his own sin. In our defensiveness and self-justification, we often cannot hear truth that comes head on. But stories get around our defenses and, if well told, turn on the light in our lives. David's beautiful response of confession and restoration is found in Psalm 51. But of course there were consequences—that baby died as a result of the sin.

Messengers sometimes tell stories that often at first don't appear to have meaning to the recipient. But as the story is winsomely shared, the message becomes clear.

Recently I have discovered great truth and redemption in the fictional stories of such authors as Charles Martin, Cathy Gohlke, Tessa Afshar, Christa Parrish, Cynthia Ruchti, Sharon Garlough Brown, and Cindy Sproles. Using stories and parables are still powerful ways to communicate truth.

Share Your Story through Proclamation

Where do we most often see the word *messenger* in the Bible? As angels!

The regular Hebrew word for *messenger* is *mal'akh*, and the Greek is *aggelos*. This may be a human messenger or a messenger of God, an angel. The context must decide the right translation.

Perhaps the most prevalent angel messages are "fear not" and "behold!"

Gabriel was the angel messenger God sent to a seemingly ordinary young teenager named Mary, proclaiming she would give birth to the Messiah. "Gabriel appeared to her and said, 'Greetings, favored woman! The Lord is with you!' . . . 'Don't be afraid, Mary,' the angel told her, "for you have found favor with God! You will conceive and give birth to a son, and you will name him Jesus. He will be very great and will be called the Son of the Most High" (Luke 1:28–32).

Sometimes our messages are proclamations—statements of what is true, what is going to happen, or reminders of God's promises. The can be encouraging, revealing, or challenging.

Often we as messengers are sent to others to call them into being what God created them to be. To affirm or draw out of them gifting and opportunities God has provided for them to live out their own unique story.

Mary's response to Gabriel was, "But how can this happen? I am a virgin" (v. 34). And Gabriel's proclamation was simply, "For nothing will be impossible with God" (v. 37 ESV).

Where in your life do you need to hear the proclamation *nothing is impossible with God*? Remember, "The message God delivered through angels has always stood firm" (Hebrews 2:2).

Remembering this promise, I cried with I finished Bob Goff's book *Everybody Always* because I didn't want the stories to end. This author—through sharing his story—proclaimed to me that he believes Lucinda McDowell can not only learn how to love widely but can *become* love.

At the end of the book Goff informed readers his message was really an intervention and that everyone I know has been calling him and asking him to break some news to me: I can no longer be the person I've been. And he asks, "What are you going to let go of? . . . Who have you been playing it safe with, while politely keeping your distance? Who has been mean or rude or flat wrong or creeps you out? Don't tell them all your opinion; give them all your love."[6]

To me that was like saying, "Nothing is impossible with God. You can do it, Cindy! God can turn you into love."

Will you find creative ways to proclaim God's great good news?

Share Your Story through Pointing

I want to be a messenger who always points to Jesus. Not in a finger-in-your-face kind-of pointing but a He-did-this-for-me-and-He-can-do-this-for-you kind-of pointing.

John the Baptist is often referred to as the forerunner—the one who opened the way to the one who was to come. Perhaps we are in a similar role of planting seeds of faith.

> This messenger was John the Baptist. He was in the wilderness and preached that people should be baptized to show that they had repented of their sins and turned to God to be forgiven.
>
> —Mark 1:4
>
> God sent a man, John the Baptist, to tell about the light so that everyone might believe because of his testimony. John himself was not the light; he was simply a witness to tell about the light.
>
> —John 1:6–8

Do you know who you are and who you aren't? John was unique—some might even say a strange character. He clothed himself in animal skins and ate locusts. But he knew what He was called to do—point to the true light of Jesus. God had appointed him to announce the arrival of Jesus, just as was prophesied in Malachi 3:1, "Look! I am sending my messenger, and he will prepare the way before me."

It is a serious responsibility to be a messenger, friends. And we should take our calling seriously—ourselves, not so much.

Know who you are—one who points. *To Jesus.* You are God's beloved. And your words can be a beautiful reflection of God's light that has come into the world.

Every time we share our story of when God's faithfulness intersected with our predicament, we are in essence communicating, "If He did this for me, then He will be there for you too!" We may not have answers or solutions to everyone's problems, but through our testimony—our story—we can point others to the one who does.

Family Legacy

Another important reason to share stories is to pass along our family legacy.

Research has shown that children who know their family history—things like where their grandparents grew up or how their parents met—have a stronger sense of control over their lives. In fact, the more a child knows about their family history, research tells us, the better their emotional health and sense of personal satisfaction. Turns out, telling our family stories is actually helpful for increasing our child's self-confidence.[7]

I will teach you hidden lessons from our past—stories we have heard and known, stories our ancestors handed down to us. We will not hide these truths from our children; we will tell the next generation about the glorious deeds of the LORD, about his power and his mighty wonders.

—Psalm 78:2–4

Author Shelly Wildman offers three key reasons to share stories with the next generation:

1. So our kids will have hope: The hope the Bible talks about is not a fleeting hope—it's a hope set on God. This is the kind of hope that lasts.

2. So they won't forget God's "glorious miracles": Tell your kids about all the ways God has shown up for you. These aren't coincidences—they're miracles!

3. So our kids will obey God's commands: When we impart our own faith, sharing in what God has done, our kids, hopefully, will want to not just *follow*, but *obey* the same trustworthy God.[8]

Take a moment to list some of the important family legacies you would like to pass along to the younger generation.

_____

_____

_____

_____

The Rest of the Story

A messenger obeys the calling. Like Ezekiel, we are to share stories whether or not our words are heard or read. Really? Yes, really.

Because nothing is wasted with God. Seeds planted deep down may eventually become seeds harvested. That's not our concern. Our job is obedience. God's job is the fruit.

As your *soul strong* life embodies the seven keys laid out in this book, the fruit *will* come. But it may not look at all like you hoped or expected.

I've shared my own *soul strong* journey because I want you to know that God is at the center of our lives. Yes, the story I opened this section with is a bit intense, but honestly, it's not even the hardest or most dramatic story of my life journey. Allow me to do a follow-up to that introduction.

The ten years following my opening story were a roller coaster. On my fifth anniversary I gave birth to our fourth child, Maggie, and rejoiced in our growing family. But just before I turned forty, I was diagnosed as clinically depressed—brought on by too many changes too quickly and physiological complications. It took a village—medically, emotionally, spiritually—to restore my health. However that journey gave me increased compassion and empathy for others flailing in darkness. Mike and I spent that first decade working hard on our marriage and parenting. Through it all God ushered me through an intense one-on-one grace tutorial resulting in a transformation from a striving hot mess to an already-accepted and beloved daughter. Not perfect, mind you, just radically and totally different.

Rather than jumping higher, I began to soar.

As a lifelong learner I keep discovering more and more of God and all He has called me to be and do. Telling my story in countless ways has been the overflow of living it. The first six chapters of this book reveal much of what I have learned, and the companion devotional—*Life-Giving Choices: 60 Days to What Matters Most*—spells out specific daily choices women can make in order to live in serenity and strength. Because our choices matter.

My life today is rich and rare. Last year I celebrated thirty-five years of marriage to the only man I've ever loved. Our six young adult children (the girls' marriages brought new sons) are all thriving personally and professionally, and our four remarkable grandchildren delight us no end. The best part? They still want to come visit!

I'll readily admit that this season of life has its own set of challenges. But whenever Mike and I need extra strength, wisdom, perseverance, or hope, we have a lifetime of spiritual soul deposits from which to make a withdrawal.

For more than forty-five years I have intentionally shared my story—at times so vulnerable I wanted to take back the words as soon as I spoke, published, or posted. But my authenticity opened doors to speak into hearts, listen, and pray. And today I have to pinch myself to realize I am writing these words in my fifteenth published book.

One of my passions is in helping others communicate through writing and speaking, so I spend much of my ministry investing in younger writers and speakers through serving on faculty of conferences and through co-directing *reNEW—retreat for New England Writing and Speaking*. I find it humbling, to say the least, to share all I've learned since I thought I knew it all. And I'm still growing.

Soul Strong to the End

There is so much we still don't know or understand about life. My seven keys for a *soul strong* life are limited, as I know only so well. But they are a beginning. And I believe whenever we set our faces like a flint to do God's will, we will never be ashamed (Isaiah 50:7 NIV).

One day we will know the ending of the story as we are lovingly embraced by the Storyteller. "For now we see only a reflection as in a mirror; then we shall see face to face. Now I know in part; then I shall know fully, even as I am fully known" (1 Corinthians 13:12 NIV).

Only then will we fully understand what all those promises meant and how our lives had meaning and purpose. Can't you just imagine that reunion?

> Stories to tell, griefs to share, joys to celebrate. Some of us are walking, others limping, and some leaping. Though we are scarred and maimed from our trials and battles, though we are weary and wounded, we are more beautiful than ever, anticipating living out the grandest happily ever after of all time.[9]

I have often thought that the essence of our life stories is most beautifully described by C. S. Lewis at the end of his Chronicles of Narnia series in which he brings everyone together in the closing of *The Last Battle.* Peter, Edmund, Lucy, and all the others go "further up and further in," where they see Aslan the lion who has been the Christ figure throughout the series. As all gather in a grand reunion, he leaps down the mountain to greet them and says that there was a real railway accident, and they are all now in the Shadowlands—dead.

> The dream is ended; this is the morning! And as He spoke, He no longer looked to them like a lion; but the things that began to happen after that were so great and beautiful that I cannot write them . . . For them it was only the beginning of the real story. All their life in this world and all their adventures in Narnia had only been the cover and the title page: Now at last they were beginning Chapter One of the Great Story in which no one on earth has read: which goes on forever: in which every chapter is better than the one before.[10]

> Then I heard the Lord asking, "Whom should I send as a messenger to this people? Who will go for us?" I said, *"Here I am. Send me."*
>
> —Isaiah 6:8 (emphasis added)

Why Do You Do It?

I had just finished writing this book, recalling Lewis's "further up and further in" and typing, "Here I am. Send me," when word came that my dear friend and colleague in ministry—Jennifer Kennedy Dean—had died quite suddenly.

In the midst of shock, disbelief, then tears of grief and sadness, I wondered at the meaning of this loss to the world. Jennifer's passion was drawing people to Jesus and encouraging them to live a praying life. She was one of the wisest in-depth Bible teachers I have ever known. She was devoted to her sons, daughters-in-law, and grandchildren. But Jennifer was also a precious prayer partner and friend to me. We were exactly the same age.

And she died doing what God called her to do—pouring truth and grace into the lives of those around her. What kept this *soul strong* woman going, especially after her young husband's untimely death? Perhaps it was remembering that one day, long ago, she said yes to God and began a journey into life as God's beloved daughter.

I've thought often about this question—*why* do I do it? I believe I've chosen to allow God to use me as a voice of encouragement simply by saying yes to the vibrant life Christ died to offer me. Each morning I look into the mirror and say, "Cindy, you are a daughter of the King—now live like it!"

My mandate comes from Paul's words in Romans 8:15–17 (*The Message*):

> This resurrection life you received from God is not a timid, grave-tending life. It's adventurously expectant, greeting God with a childlike "What's next, Papa?" God's Spirit touches our spirits and confirms who we really are. We know who he is, and we know who we are: Father and children. And we know we are going to

get what's coming to us—an unbelievable inheritance! We go through exactly what Christ goes through. If we go through the hard times with him, then we're certainly going to go through the good times with him!

Christ's love compels me (2 Corinthians 5:14 NIV). Because of all He did, through love of me, how could I not respond in obedience and love—sharing with others such good news? A dozen years ago I adopted a personal mission statement: *To glorify God and live in His grace and freedom and, through the power of the Holy Spirit, to use my gifts to communicate God's faithfulness, extend His grace, and encourage others to trust Him fully.*

The end of life here on earth can come very suddenly, as I have witnessed over and over this past year. How important it is to believe that our only hope is, as the Heidelberg Catechism states, "That I am not my own but belong with body and soul, both in life and in death, to my faithful Saviour Jesus Christ."

Sister, Christ calls you too. Please know that every word in the Bible is for all. Christ's final words before His ascension remind me of three reasons why I seek to live a *soul strong* life.

I have been given all authority in heaven and on earth. Therefore, *go and make disciples* of all the nations, baptizing them in the name of the Father and the Son and the Holy Spirit. *Teach these new disciples to obey all the commands* I have given you. And be sure of this: *I am with you always*, even to the end of the age.

—Matthew 28:18–20 (emphasis added)

Called to TRAIN: Jesus begins what we call the Great Commission with a reminder that in the authority of God the Father, and through the power of the Holy Spirit, He is calling His faithful to "go and make disciples." The root word for *disciple* is from the Latin *discipulus*, which can mean "learner" or "pupil." It means we follow Jesus. Thus I walk through those open doors and invest in people, helping them understand spiritual disciplines and grow deeper in their walk of faith.

Called to TEACH: Jesus emphasizes that we are to "teach these new disciples to obey all the commands." We discover what those are by fully knowing God's Word and helping to unfold its meaning to others so they might embrace the wisdom these words offer to every circumstance of life today. My response is to know, to obey, and to teach others all that has been revealed to me.

Called to TRUST: The best part of all is that I can "be sure of this"—Jesus is with me always. I can fully trust the sovereignty and goodness of the One of knows me best and loves me most. This frees me to live my life in such a way that expresses a deep trust and glorifies my Creator, Sustainer, and Redeemer. I can live *soul strong* because I am never alone.

We are not our own when we belong to Jesus Christ. We go where He sends us and obey what He commands. Often at great price. But also for great reward—the hope of heaven. Who knows what fruit will be sown from our short life story?

Soul Strong

That day I turned around, and life had flown . . .

Whilst chasing dreams and children;

Both stumbling and soaring

in the search for holy significance.

Compassionately rescued from despair;

Gifted with a grace that accepts and extends;

Encouraged and loved.

Discovering serenity in silence,

and strength in surrender.

Filled, then poured out.

Heart broken, then mended.

Embracing creative words, life-giving music,

breathtaking beauty, and extraordinary people.

Walking with a limp but still walking

Daily in God's presence and power.

Beloved.

Learning to love everybody always.

Not a perfect life, more a passionate pursuit.

Here is what I know for sure:

We can live *soul strong.*

—Lucinda Secrest McDowell

About the Author

Lucinda Secrest McDowell, MTS, is passionate about embracing life—both through deep soul care and by living courageously to touch a needy world. A storyteller who engages both heart and mind, she delights in *helping you choose a life of serenity and strength.* A graduate of Gordon-Conwell Theological Seminary and Furman University, McDowell is the author of fifteen books and contributing author to more than thirty books, including *Life-Giving Choices, Dwelling Places, Ordinary Graces, Live These Words,* and *Refresh!* She is a member of the Redbud Writers Guild and Advanced Writers and Speakers Association. Her books have received numerous awards, and Lucinda received the Mount Hermon Writer of the Year award. She guest blogs for The Write Conversation, Blue Ridge Mountains Christian Writers Conference, and (in)courage.

Whether codirecting *reNEW—retreat for New England Writing and Speaking,* pouring into young mamas, serving on faculty for writing and speaking conferences, or leading a restorative day of prayer, she is energized by investing in people of all ages. Lucinda's favorites include creative words, tea parties, good books, laughing friends, ancient prayers, country music, cozy quilts, musical theatre, and especially her family, scattered around the world doing amazing things. Known for her ability to convey deep truth in practical and winsome ways, she writes from her home, "Sunnyside" cottage, in New England and and shares words at LucindaSecrestMcDowell.com.

> Every word you give me is a miracle word—how could I help but obey? Break open your words, let the light shine out, let ordinary people see the meaning.
>
> —Psalm 119:129–130 *The Message*

Mission: To glorify God and live in His grace and freedom and through the power of the Holy Spirit to use my gifts to communicate God's faithfulness, extend His grace, and encourage others to trust Him fully.

Let's Stay Connected!
Website/Blog: www.LucindaSecrestMcDowell.com
E-mail: LucindaSMcDowell@gmail.com
Phone: 860-402-9551
Twitter: @LucindaSMcDowel
Instagram: @LucindaSecrestMcDowell
Facebook: Author/Speaker Lucinda Secrest McDowell
Mail: Encouraging Words, P.O. Box 290707, Wethersfield CT 06129 USA

Gratitudes

I am not naturally strong. But my life thus far continues to echo the psalmist's boast, "On the day I called, you answered me; my *strength of soul* you increased" (Psalm 138:3 ESV, emphasis added). So if I have anything to say to you at all, it is that God is right here, providing everything we need. Always.

It has been for me both a humbling and hope-filled experience to spend this past year looking for the fingerprints of God on my life thus far and wrestling with how to condense the meaning, purpose, and practice of a vibrant life into seven short chapters. Someone once remarked that as we grow older our litany of response can be reduced to one phrase, repeated often—*Thank you. Thank you. Thank you.*

I agree. Thus I conclude this volume with those words to both God, my Heavenly Father, and to you, my faithful readers.

Thank you for seeking to live a *soul strong* life in order to live authentically and love outrageously! While your investment in reading this book thrills me as the author, what is far more important are your efforts to honor God, serve others, and leave a legacy of grace and joy to a fractured world.

I feel quite grateful to each person who takes time to read my scribbled words or listen to my spoken words. I take my calling seriously—myself, not so much. As God keeps opening doors, I hope to see you soon for a hug, conversation, or hot cup of tea.

Special thanks go to John Herring, Ramona Richards, Tina Atchenson, Meredith Dunn, Reagan Jackson, Charissa Newell, Bradley Isbell, Randy Herring, the wonderful sales team, and the entire staff at New Hope Publishers and

Iron Stream Media for so graciously embracing the message of *Soul Strong* and helping to get this volume into your hands today.

I felt very vulnerable as I prayerfully entrusted some brilliant younger women I admire to read my work in progress and give me feedback and wisdom along the way. To those *soul strong* women, I thank you for helping to make this a better book—Amy, Arlene, Carrye, Heidi, Jenn, Julie, Lee, Lindsey, Lisa, Maureen, Rachel, Rebecca, Sharon, Tammy, Teri Lynne, and Tracy.

Thanks to all the *soul strong* women from the past whose words and lives continue to call me to live my own story with commitment and courage. These spiritual mothers—saints and sinners, just like me—continue to set the bar high.

Thank you to those who daily encourage and pray for me, especially my best friend Maggie. I'm also grateful to the hospitality of Betsy and Marty for *La Coquille*—a sanctuary where many of these words were birthed.

I send special thanks to the amazing women in these treasured communities of which I am a part: SpaSisters (you know who you are, and what would I do without you?); Redbud Writers Guild; my *reNEW—retreat for New England Writing and Speaking* community (Rachel and others); Daybreak prayer group (Karen, Judy, and Jessica); growth group (Kathy, Helga, Vickie, and Colette); writers' prayer group (Tessa and Lauren); Tuesday night Bible study; Wednesday First Place Zoom Bible study; and my Advanced Writers and Speakers Association (AWSA) colleagues.

Special thank you to my ninety-two-year old Mama—Sarah Hasty Secrest. I would not be who I am today without your strength, soul, and sacrifice. Also my sisters Cathy and Susan and my sisters-of-the-heart Maggie and Claire—you are always there for me. Thank you for your unconditional acceptance of this flawed human who loves you all. A big shout-out to all the strong women kinfolk in clans McDowell, Secrest, Hasty, van Seventer, Karpoff, and Stallings—especially my two favorite Aunts Carol and Rebecca.

I'm especially thankful for my two *soul strong* daughters—Fiona and Maggie—to whom I dedicate this book. Thank you for listening, loving, and still embracing me in your lives. You are most certainly the most important gift

I leave to a world I will never see. I am confident God has His hand on your lives and your unique stories and that the world is a better place because of the beautiful, brilliant, and brave women you are.

As always my immediate family is my greatest source of encouragement and joy. Gigantic gratitudes to my husband Mike, who has loved me well for thirty-six years, and to Justin, Tim, Fiona, Tim K, Saoirse, Hugh, Bram, Stephen, Maggie, and Thomas. You are indeed my most important legacy.

Jesus, lover of my soul. Thank You for the unconditional love, grace, goodness, forgiveness, new beginnings, severe mercies, wonder, joy, provision, promises kept, strength, music, and moments. "You make known to me the path of life; in your presence there is fullness of joy; at your right hand are pleasures forevermore" (Psalm 16:11 ESV).

Lucinda Secrest McDowell

"Sunnyside"
Wethersfield, Connecticut

Notes

Chapter 1: Live Loved

[1] Henri Nouwen, *You Are the Beloved: Daily Mediations for Spiritual Living*, comp. and ed. Gabrielle Earnshaw (New York: Convergent Books, 2017), 97.

[2] Charles Martin, *What If It's True? A Storyteller's Journey with Jesus* (Nashville, TN: W Publishing, 2019), 241.

[3] Lysa TerKeurst, *Uninvited: Living Loved When You Feel Less Than, Left Out, and Lonely* (Nashville, TN: Nelson Books, 2016), 40.

[4] Frederick Buechner, *The Magnificent Defeat* (New York: HarperCollins, 1966), 135.

[5] It took almost a decade longer than I had hoped, but after God pruned me and sent me on all kinds of perilous adventures of learning how to trust Him, I did finally find the love of my life in my thirties. We have now been married thirty-six years and have raised four children who are truly remarkable humans. While ours is not a perfect love, may I encourage you from the bottom of my heart that it is always worth waiting for God's timing in all things, including relationships.

[6] George Herbert, "Love," in *The Life and Writings of the Rev. George Herbert: With the Synagogue, an Imitation of Herbert* (Boston and Cambridge: James Munroe and Company, 1851), 272.

[7] Ruth Haley Barton, *Longing for More: A Woman's Path to Transformation in Christ* (Downers Grove IL: IVP Books, 2007), 36.

[8] William Temple, in *Classic Prayers for Every Kind*, ed. Donna K. Maltese (Uhrichsville, OH: 2017), 136.

Chapter 2: Be Authentic

[1] Elizabeth B., "Rachel Hollis and the Dangers of Curated Imperfection," *Houston Moms Blog*, December 11, 2018, https://houston.citymomsblog.com /rachel-hollis-and-the-dangers-of-curated-imperfection/.

[2] Eugene Petersen, *Leap Over a Wall: Earthly Spirituality for Everyday Christians* (New York City: HarperCollins, 1997), 42.

[3] Ibid.

[4] A. J. Drenth, "ENFJ Personality Type Profile," accessed July 15, 2019, https://personalityjunkie.com/enfj-type-profile/.

[5] Alice Fryling, "Letting Go of the False Self: How the Enneagram Can Help You Find the True You," Conversations: A Forum for Authentic Transformation (Fall/Winter 2014): 23–24, https://www.leadershiptransformations.org/documents/Enneagram%20Article-Fryling.pdf.

[6] "Personal Growth Recommendations for Enneagram Type Threes," 3: The Achiever, The Enneagram Institute, accessed July 15, 2019, https://www.enneagraminstitute.com/type-3/.

[7] Jessica Honegger, "The Paradox of Authenticity," *The Magnolia Journal,* Spring 2019, 45–46.

[8] Douglas Kaine McKelvey, "A Liturgy for the Marking of Birthdays" in *Every Moment Holy* (Nashville, TN: Rabbit Room Press, 2017), 130–132.

[9] Lucinda Secrest McDowell, *Ordinary Graces: Word Gifts for Any Season* (Nashville, TN: Abingdon Press, 2017), 32.

[10] Margot Starbuck, *Not Who I Imagined: Surprised by a Loving God* (Grand Rapids, MI: Baker Books, 2014), 21.

[11] Karen Porter, *My Place for Discovery* (Galveston TX: First Place for Health, 2018), 43.

[12] Barton, *Longing for More*, 44.

[13] Joanna Gaines, "A Note from Jo on Authenticity," Magnolia (blog), February 11, 2019, https://magnolia.com/a-note-from-jo-on-authenticity/.

[14] Ken Shigematsu, *Survival Guide for the Soul: How to Flourish Spiritually in a World that Pressures Us to Achieve* (Grand Rapids, MI: Zondervan, 2018), 180.

[15] Timothy Keller, *Counterfeit Gods: The Empty Promises of Money, Sex, and Power, and the Only Hope That Matters* (New York: Penguin, 2009), xx.

[16] Emily P. Freeman, *The Next Right Thing: A Simple, Soulful Practice for Making Life Decisions* (Grand Rapids, MI: Revell, 2019), 217, 220.

[17] Brennan Manning, *The Ragamuffin Gospel* (Sisters, OR: Multnomah Publishers, 2000), 139.

[18] Mark Labberton, *Called: The Crisis and the Promise of Following Jesus Today* (Downers Grove, IL: IVP Books, 2014), 45.

[19] Adapted from Shirley Giles Davis, *God. Gifts. You. Your Unique Calling and Design* (self-published workbook, 2018), 25.

[20] Shigematsu, *Survival Guide for the Soul*, 186.

[21] Davis, *God. Gifts. You.* 25.

[22] Adapted from Davis, *God. Gifts. You.* 15.

[23] Madeleine L'Engle, *Walking on Water: Reflections on Faith and Art* (New York: Bantam Books, 1982), 62.

[24] Ibid., 61–62.

[25] "The Methodist Covenant Service," in *Protestant Nonconformist Texts*, ed. David M. Thompson, vol. 4 (Eugene, OR: Wipf and Stock, 2015), 142.

Chapter 3: Dwell Deep

[1] Ruth Haley Barton, *Sacred Rhythms: Arranging Our Lives for Spiritual Transformation* (Downers Grove, IL: InterVarsity Press, 2006), 24.

[2] Ruth Haley Barton, "From Discipline to Desire," *Beyond Words* (blog), Transforming Center, November 23, 2005, https://transformingcenter.org/2005/11/from-desire-to-discipline/.

[3] Kevin DeYoung, *Crazy Busy: A (Mercifully) Short Book about a (Really) Big Problem* (Wheaton, IL: Crossway, 2013), 115.

[4] Ibid., 118.

[5] Adapted from Lucinda Secrest McDowell, *Dwelling Places: Words to Live in Every Season* (Nashville, TN: Abingdon Press, 2016), 273–277.

[6] Peter Scazzero, *Emotionally Healthy Spirituality: Unleash a Revolution in Your Life in Christ* (Nashville, TN: Thomas Nelson, 2006), 196.

[7] Natasha Sistrunk Robinson, *Mentor for Life: Finding Purpose through Intentional Discipleship* (Grand Rapids, MI: Zondervan, 2016), PDF e-book.

[8] Dr. Caroline Leaf, *Switch on Your Brain: The Key to Peak Happiness, Thinking, and Health* (Grand Rapids, MI: Baker Books, 2013), PDF e-book.

[9] Mckelvey, "A Liturgy for Arriving at the Ocean," in *Every Moment Holy,* 67.

[10] Michelle DeRusha, *True You: Letting Go of Your False Self to Uncover the Person God Created* (Grand Rapids, MI: Baker Books, 2019), 122.

[11] Henry Cloud and John Townsend, *Safe People: How to Find Relationships That Are Good for You* (Grand Rapids, MI: Zondervan, 1995), 143.

[12] John Ortberg, *Soul Keeping: Caring for the Most Important Part of You* (Grand Rapids, MI: Zondervan, 2014), 140.

[13] Saint Aidan of Lindisfarne, "Prayer of St. Aidan of Lindisfarne" in *The Ancient Faith Prayer Book*, comp. and ed. Vassilios Papavassiliou (Chesterton, IN: Ancient Faith Publishing, 2014), 139.

[14] Barbara Mahany, *The Blessings of Motherprayer: Sacred Whispers of Mothering* (Nashville, TN: Abingdon Press, 2018), 127.

[15] C. S. Lewis, *Mere Christianity* (New York: Touchstone, 1996), 183.

[16] Thomas Kelly, as quoted in *Prayer: Finding the Heart's True Home* by Richard Foster (San Francisco: Harper San Francisco, 1992), 125.

[17] Foster, *Prayer*, 127.

[18] Ruth Myers, *A Treasury of Praise: Enjoying God Anew* (Colorado Springs, CO: Multnomah Books, 2007), 13–14.

Chapter 4: Pray Always

[1] Jennifer Kennedy Dean, *Set Apart: A Six-Week Study of the Beatitudes* (Birmingham, AL: New Hope Publishers, 2015), 161.

[2] Foster, *Prayer*, 11–12.

[3] Robert Benson, *Daily Prayer: A Little Book for Saying the Daily Office* (Raleigh, NC: Carolina Broadcasting and Publishing Inc., 2006), 9.

[4] John Baillie, *A Diary of Private Prayer* (New York: Charles Scribner's Sons, 1949), 41.

[5] Amy Carmichael, "For Our Children," in *Mountain Breezes: The Collected Poems of Amy Carmichael* (Fort Washington, PA: Christian Life Crusade, 1999), 149–150.

[6] Stormie Omartian, *The Power of Praying for Your Adult Children* (Eugene, OR: Harvest House Publishers, 2014), PDF e-book.

[7] Foster, *Prayer*, 120.

[8] Jennifer Kennedy Dean, *SEEK: 28 Days to Extraordinary Prayer* (Birmingham, AL: New Hope Publishers, 2019), 3.

[9] Kurt Bjorklund, *Prayers for Today: A Yearlong Journey of Contemplative Prayer* (Chicago: Moody Publishers, 2011), 13–14.

[10] John Stott, in "John Stott's Morning Trinitarian Prayer" by Trevin Wax, *The Gospel Coalition* (blog), March 21, 2010, https://www.thegospelcoalition.org/blogs/trevin-wax/john-stotts-morning-trinitarian-prayer/.

[11] Saint Augustine, in *Catholic Prayers for All Occasions,* ed. Jacquelyn Lindsey (Huntington, IN: Our Sunday Visitor Publishing Division, 2017), PDF e-book.

[12] Bjorklund, *Prayers for Today*, 180.

[13] William Barclay, *A Barclay Prayer Book* (Louisville: Westminster John Knox Press, 2003), 134–135.

[14] Frank Colquhoun, in *Prayers for People Under Pressure* by Jonathan Aitken (Wheaton, IL: Crossway Books, 2008), 204.

[15] Abraham Lincoln, "A Proclamation, for a day of national humiliation, fasting and prayer!" Published 1863, Boston, MA, accessed September 10, 2019, https://www.loc.gov/resource/lprbscsm.scsm0265/?st=text.

[16] Peter Sutcliffe, in *The Celtic Resource Book* by Martin Wallace (London: Church House Publishing, 2009), 37.

[17] Rachel Britton, "Being Bold in God's Presence," Rachel Britton (blog), accessed September 10, 2019, https://rachelbritton.com/mercy-words/.

Chapter 5: Overcome Pain

[1] Joni and Friends Inc., *Infinite Hope in the Midst of Struggles* (Carol Stream, IL: Tyndale House Publishers, 2018), viii.

[2] Ibid.

[3] Barton, *Longing for More*, 181.

[4] Ken Gire, *Shaped by the Cross: Meditations on the Sufferings of Jesus* (Downers Grove, IL: IVP Books, 2011), PDF e-book.

[5] Mary Witkowski, "Franny Crosby," Bridgeport Library History Center, accessed September 18, 2019, https://bportlibrary.org/hc/heroes-and-villains/fanny-crosby/.

[6] Elisabeth Elliot, *Suffering Is Never for Nothing* (Nashville, TN: B&H Publishing, 2019), 92–93.

[7] Ibid., 94.

[8] Amy Carmichael, "Constant Victory," in *Mountain Breezes*, 274.

[9] Tammy Sue Willey, *Wounded Song* (self-published, 2017), 302.

[10] David Powlison, *God's Grace in Your Suffering* (Wheaton, IL: Crossway, 2018), 91.

[11] Malcolm Muggeridge, in *Conformed to His Image: Biblical and Practical Approaches to Spiritual Formation* by Kenneth D. Boa (Grand Rapids, MI: Zondervan, 2001), 457.

[12] Jane Grayshorn, "In Times of Pain," in *Prayers for People Under Pressure* by Jonathan Aitken (Wheaton, IL: Crossway Books, 2008), 196.

[13] Michael Card, *A Sacred Sorrow: Reaching Out to God in the Lost Language of Lament* (Colorado Springs, CO: NavPress, 2005), 29.

[14] Barton, *Longing for More*, 183.

[15] Les Parrott, *You're Stronger Than You Think: The Power to Do What You Feel You Can't* (Carol Stream, IL: Tyndale House Publishers Inc., 2012), 131.

[16] Joni and Friends Inc., *Infinite Hope*, 116.

[17] Janet Holm McHenry, *The Complete Guide to the Prayers of Jesus* (Minneapolis, MN: Bethany House Publishers, 2018), 147.

[18] Cynthia Fantasia, *In the Lingering Light: Courage and Hope for the Alzheimer's Caregiver* (Colorado Springs, CO: NavPress, 2019), 122.

[19] Ibid., 135.

[20] Ibid., 34.

Chapter 6: Extend Kindness

[1] Paula Spencer Scott, "Let's Make 2017 the Year of Being Kind," *Parade*, December 30, 2016, https://parade.com/534041/paulaspencer/lets-make-2017-the-year-of-being-kind/.

[2] Krista Tippett, "Sylvia Boorstein: What We Nurture," *On Being with Krista Tippett*, aired May 5, 2011, https://onbeing.org/programs/sylvia-boorstein-what-we-nurture/.

[3] Ann Voskamp, *The Way of Abundance: A 60-Day Journey into a Deeply Meaningful Life* (Grand Rapids, MI: Zondervan, 2018), 133–134.

[4] Robinson, *Mentor for Life*, PDF e-book.

[5] Bob Goff, in "Bob Goff Shares the Secret to Loving Difficult People" by Andre Henry, *Relevant*, April 16, 2018, https://relevantmagazine.com/culture/bob-goff-shares-secret-loving-difficult-people/.

[6] Bob Goff, in "Kissing the Witch Doctor: What Love Does (with Bob Goff)" by Wendy Cloherty, *ViewPoint*, March 20, 2015, https://viewpoint.pointloma.edu/kissing-the-witch-doctor-what-love-does-with-bob-goff/.

[7] Bob Goff, *Everybody Always: Becoming Love in a World Full of Setbacks and Difficult People* (Nashville, TN: Nelson Books, 2018), 218–219.

[8] Shannan Martin, *The Ministry of Ordinary Places: Waking Up to God's Goodness Around You* (Nashville, TN: Nelson Books, 2018), 119.

[9] Robert Benson, *A Good Life: Benedict's Guide to Everyday Joy* (Brewster, MA: Paraclete Press, 2005), 66–67.

[10] Martin, *What If It's True?*, 249–250.

[11] Barry Corey, *Love Kindness: Discover the Power of a Forgotten Christian Virtue* (Carol Stream, IL: Tyndale House Publishers Inc., 2019), 94.

[12] Carrye Burr, *How to be a Moon: Embrace Your Worth. Reflect God. Light Up Your Generation.* (Self-published, 2018), 77.

[13] Foster, *Prayer*, 255.

[14] Lori Stanley Roeleveld, *The Art of Hard Conversations: Biblical Tools for the Tough Talks That Matter* (Grand Rapids, MI: Kregel Publications, 2019), 172.

[15] Ibid., 173.

[16] Ibid., 110.

[17] McKelvey, "A Liturgy for Serving Others," in *Every Moment Holy,* 155–156.

[18] Ken Gire, in Borklund, *Prayers for Today*, PDF e-book.

[19] L'Engle, *Walking on Water*, 122.

Chapter 7: Share Stories

[1] Heather A. Berlin and Christof Koch, "Defense Mechanisms: Neuroscience Meets Psychoanalysis," *Scientific American*, April 1, 2009, https://www.scientificamerican.com/article/neuroscience-meets-psychoanalysis/.

[2] Dan B. Allender and Lisa K. Fann, *To Be Told: God Invites You to Coauthor Your Future* Workbook (Colorado Springs: WaterBrook Press, 2005), 6.

[3] Allender and Fann, *To Be Told* Workbook, 2–3.

[4] Lisa M. Hendey, *I Am God's Storyteller* (Brewster, MA: Paraclete Press, 2019), 6.

[5] Os Guinness, *Fool's Talk: Recovering the Art of Christian Persuasion* (Downers Grove, IL: InterVarsity Press, 2015), 174–175.

[6] Goff, *Everybody Always*, 218

[7] Shelly Wildman, "Tell Me a Story" Shelly Wildman (blog), accessed September 18, 2019, https://www.shellywildman.com/blog-1/tell-me-a-story?fbclid=IwAR2OSNS8O_kuqzUw8O0ve9Kd8YADySxb-LHmc6TiAdzlpRbHnKYaopJWvMM.

[8] Ibid.

[9] Nicole Johnson, *Keeping a Princess Heart: In a Not-So-Fairy-Tale World* (Nashville, TN: Thomas Nelson, 2003), 181.

[10] C. S. Lewis, *The Last Battle* (New York: Penguin Books, 1956), 165.

**If you enjoyed this book, will you consider sharing
the message with others?**

Let us know your thoughts at info@newhopepublishers.com.
You can also let the author know by visiting or sharing a photo of the
cover on our social media pages or leaving a review at a retailer's site.
All of it helps us get the message out!

Twitter.com/NewHopeBooks
Facebook.com/NewHopePublishers
Instagram.com/NewHopePublishers

———————

New Hope® Publishers, Ascender Books, Iron Stream Books,
and New Hope Kidz are imprints of Iron Stream Media,
which derives its name from Proverbs 27:17,

"As iron sharpens iron, so one person sharpens another."

This sharpening describes the process of discipleship,
one to another. With this in mind, Iron Stream Media provides
a variety of solutions for churches, ministry leaders, and nonprofits
ranging from in-depth Bible study curriculum and Christian book
publishing to custom publishing and consultative services. Through the
popular Life Bible Study and Student Life Bible Study brands,
ISM provides web-based full-year and short-term Bible study
teaching plans as well as printed devotionals, Bibles, and
discipleship curriculum.

For more information on ISM and
New Hope Publishers,
please visit

IronStreamMedia.com
NewHopePublishers.com

Your daily choices matter.

Learn to choose opportunities that are life-giving.

Available from NewHopePublishers.com or your favorite retailer.

You may also enjoy . . .

PENNY COOKE

Pursuing Prayer

BEING EFFECTIVE IN A BUSY WORLD

"With the heart of a gentle encourager, Lucinda Secrest McDowell provides practical wisdom for how to live a vibrant life, rooted and grounded in God's extravagant love and grace. *Soul Strong* is a generous offering from an honest, trustworthy mentor. I'm grateful for this beautiful gift."

—**Sharon Garlough Brown,**
author of the *Sensible Shoes Series* and
Shades of Light

"The first time I met Lucinda Secrest McDowell she looked me straight in the eyes as asked me how she could pray for me. I knew then I'd encountered someone who genuinely cares for others and desires to see God move in their lives and work. In *Soul Strong*, we are all the beneficiaries of that same supportive spirit one receives when sitting with Lucinda at a conference or a coffee shop. This beautiful blend of biblical truth, personal wisdom, and practical guidance will help any women who wants to live the full, vibrant life Jesus promises us."

—**Teri Lynne Underwood,**
author of *Praying for Girls: Asking God for the*
Things They Need Most

"Each day we are faced with choices that determine our posture and stamina as we run the race Jesus has laid out for His own. In *Soul Strong*, Lucinda Secrest McDowell tracks right alongside and lovingly points us to the Word of God and seven decisions we must make to run with steadfastness and joy. Dig in, do the work, and watch your soul strength rise."

—**Lee Nienhuis,**
author of *Brave Mom, Brave Kids*
and host of the Moms in Prayer podcast

"Upon first meeting Lucinda Secrest McDowell I quickly sensed a vibrancy, prompting me to lean in closely to her words in *Soul Strong: 7 Keys to a Vibrant Life*. As a woman in my late thirties, I loved the practical applications and truth found in these pages as Lucinda uses her own transparency, Scripture, and stories to beautifully point you back again and again to how to live *soul strong*. The interactive format is helpful in exploring simple but life-changing keys for the reader to live a vibrant faith-filled life. If you have a longing for your soul to feel strong on the good days, bad days, and all the in-between-days, join my friend Lucinda on this compelling journey."

—Jennifer Hand,
speaker, trauma counselor, and
author of *31 Days to Coming Alive*

"At once a Bible study and a study of one's self, this amazing little book will not only fill you with hope but will inspire you to dig in deep, grow in your faith, and abide sweetly in Jesus. Filled with beautiful prayers and gentle reminders of the firm foundation we have in God, Lucinda Secrest McDowell authentically deals with challenges we face to becoming strong in our faith. *Soul Strong* is about so much more than simply doing the things that will make our souls strong—it inspires us to dwell deep in the only One who *can* make our souls strong. Intentional, biblical, encouraging, and infused with hope. I cannot recommend this book enough!"

—Heidi Chiavaroli,
Carol award-winning author of *Freedom's Ring*
and *The Tea Chest*

"Lucinda Secrest McDowell offers a beautiful invitation in *Soul Strong* to explore the real you according to God's design. She strings stories together with the Word to illustrate a beautiful vision of an authentically vibrant life shaped by deep abiding in God's love and kindness, grace and mercy, gratitude and hope."

—Elisa Pulliam, coach,
speaker, and author of *Meet the New You*
and *Unblinded Faith*

"As a wife, mom, homeschooler, and teacher, my soul has felt weary in the well-doing. Then Lucinda's *Soul Strong* came my way—and I knew this is the book so many of us desperately need. In spiritual love and wisdom, Lucinda Secrest McDowell guides us to see clearly what we often neglect: soul care. Her prayer-filled, story-rich writing guides us to set aside insecurities and entanglements and instead make rich deposits in the eternal bank of our souls. More than just inspirational, this book is foundational and practical; I read feeling deep relief at having scriptural keys to guide my way toward a stronger, more vibrant inner life with Christ."

—Julie Kieras,
family and parenting blogger
at HappyStrongHome.com

"We can spend countless hours working on externals. We apply makeup to smooth our skin and buy clothes that make us appear thinner. While there's nothing wrong with these things, there is something infinitely more important— *the soul.* Lucinda Secrest McDowell serves as a capable and caring guide into the interior. The journey toward knowing God and yourself better is well worth it. *Soul Strong: 7 Keys to a Vibrant Life* will help you grow from the inside out."

—Arlene Pellicane,
speaker and author of *Calm, Cool, and Connected: 5 Digital Habits for a More Balanced Life*

"When we wonder how to respond to all that life throws at us, *Soul Strong* gives practical and biblical guidance from real life on how to navigate the journey well. With a wealth of wisdom and encouragement to go deep with God through His Word, Lucinda Secrest McDowell invites us to explore who we are and how God wants us to live. This is not a book to flip through but rather to work through slowly, taking the time to apply the tried and tested practices to your own life. This is what I will be doing."

—Rachel Britton,
speaker, author, content director of
Radiant.NYC and co-director of *reNEW*

"*Soul Strong: 7 Keys to a Vibrant Life* is water for a thirsty soul! Lucinda Secrest McDowell masterfully weaves both personal story and practical advice together, giving valuable tools that will both strengthen and encourage each reader in their own life journey. I cannot wait to share copies with the young women I mentor."

—Tammy Gerhard,
counselor, mentor, women's ministry leader

"Through *Soul Strong*, Lucinda Secrest McDowell takes one on a powerful journey through Scripture and personal testimony to discover how to live authentically and fully in the will of God for our lives. An excellent resource for women's ministries, Bible studies, small groups, and individuals, *Soul Strong* will empower and enrich your walk with Jesus and your desire to live the life that is more than we could ask or imagine."

—Lindsey P. Brackett,
award-winning author of *Still Waters*

"Lucinda Secrest McDowell's transparent writing is rooted with Scripture and complemented with practical tips and powerful reflection questions. When I closed *Soul Strong*, I felt as though I held a guidebook in my hand, prepared to move forward in my faith, my soul stronger. I loved the interweaving of story, Scripture, practical tips, and places for journaling. I truly felt like I was walking on a path of soul-discovery with a trusted friend who is just a little farther down the road, cheering me on. This is a book I want to share with my young adult daughter. *Soul Strong* is written with such tenderness, like a letter from a loving aunt or longtime friend who truly understands the challenges and blocks to our own discovery of who God created each of us to be."

—Amy Breitmann,
radio host and author of *A God of All Seasons:*
Walking Towards Mercy, Grace and Hope